Onwards

by Karen Dudley

Onwards

by Karen Dudley

Published in 2023 by Penguin Books,
an imprint of Penguin Random House
South Africa (Pty) Ltd

Company Reg. No. 1953/000441/07

The Estuaries, 4 Oxbow Crescent, Century Avenue,
Century City 7441, Cape Town, South Africa

PO Box 1144, Cape Town, 8000, South Africa

www.penguinrandomhouse.co.za

PUBLISHER: Beverley Dodd

MANAGING EDITOR AND EDITOR: Aimee Carelse

ART DIRECTION AND DESIGN: Roxanne Spears

TYPESETTING AND DESIGN: Randall Watson

PROOFREADER AND INDEXER: Cecilia Barfield

PHOTOGRAPHER: Claire Gunn

FOOD AND PROP STYLIST: Karen Dudley

FOOD STYLIST'S ASSISTANT: Phatiswa Magazi

Reproduction: Studio Repro

Printed and bound in Hong Kong
by Golden Prosperity Ltd

ISBN 978-1-48590-114-3

Contents

Introduction

Looking at the pile of beaten pots, bowls and the well-seasoned baking trays, a little sob echoed around my quiet shop. In the slightly stale air, my vintage crockery and wobbly tables seemed to have lost their meaning. The street outside was quiet.
No hooting taxis, no car guards, no cars jostling for parking.

I understood that our lives would never be the same.

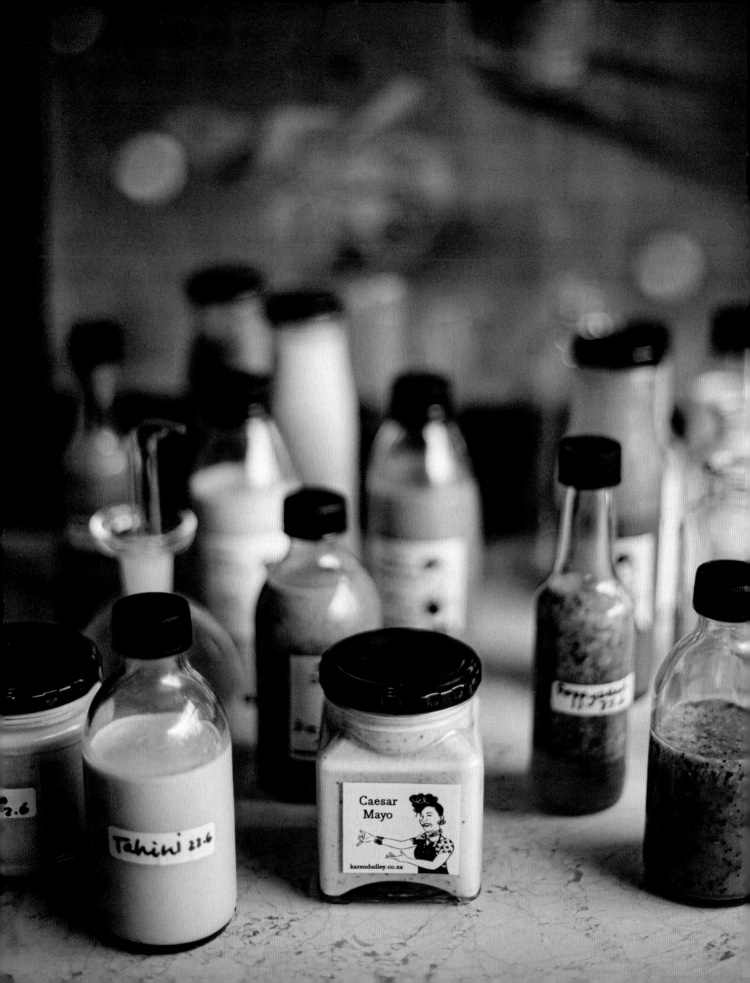

[1]

Recipes to help with letting go

My heart heavy with sorrow, my groaning home fridge filled with 5-litre buckets removed from the cold room at The Kitchen: wholegrain mustard, horseradish, capers, olives, Danish feta, tahini and anchovies. A few bags of herbs and other sundry vegetables were wedged between these giants.

I began making dressings, pickles, pestos and mayos with the steady, compulsive energy of one trained in the habit of using resources that are to hand. I could not let things go to waste.

There was a whole palette of produce to play with and I was in my zone... making-making-making... pitting one flavour against another... tasting-tasting-tasting. Listening... to the caper, to the salty anchovy, to the surprising brine. Scanning the internet for new ideas and inspiration, I was deep in the world of flavour. It was my release, my escape, my salvation! This was what I loved best: playing with flavour. I am an alchemist! Soon lots of little bottles of sauces and relishes began populating the fridge. I felt almost guilty at the relief of this exercise and the indulgence of Whipped Feta to spoon into pasta, and Caper Sultana Relish over steak.

Set against this small fervour of private industry was the weight of anxiety of taking care of my people, now hungry for not having work for months, the administration of TERS payments and Telkom, ADT, banks, the property owner – the spectral, relentless motions of my ghost restaurant. And then, the resolute letting go of stainless steel tables, fridges and ovens, my vintage shop fittings – and my savings!

I had to forego the pleasure of feeding people, of making something fresh, delicious and satisfying, daily. I needed to let go of work that had given my life shape and purpose. I got to work with people that I loved. I was a steward of produce and people.

Help and light came from all sides. Our community, which evidently existed beyond bricks and mortar, gave donations. Friends from abroad committed their Covid relief to my staff in Cape Town. Our customers bought books, ordered meals and added to our Staff Fund. I began filling bottles of dressings and sauces for rapidly expanding online platforms like UCook and Granadilla Eats, doing online cooking demonstrations and live shows for South Africans who were ready to support my people.

There was some virtue in my sauce alchemy: I was employing the well-practised habit of using what was available to me and I was committed to an exercise that brought me joy. What I began to understand, too, was that these sauces made my cooking so much more fun. And I tapped into what had always given my life purpose: creation and redemption! I could help people live simply and well. And these sauces were the way forward.

Caper Sultana Relish

½ cup sultanas

2 Tbsp white balsamic vinegar or white wine vinegar

3 cloves garlic, peeled and grated

3 Tbsp capers

6 anchovy fillets

2 Tbsp sunflower oil

1 Tbsp caper brine

40 g Italian (or curly) parsley, very finely chopped

⅓ cup extra-virgin olive oil

Salt and black pepper, to taste

Add the sultanas to a small bowl and pour over the vinegar. Leave them for about 20 minutes to plump up a little.

In a food processor, pulse the garlic, capers, anchovies and sunflower oil to a coarse paste. Add the caper brine, parsley, sultanas with vinegar, and pulse. (You want a coarse relish, so be careful not to overdo it!)

Remove the paste from the food processor, transfer to a bowl and whisk in the olive oil. Season with salt and black pepper.

MAKES 1½ CUPS

Nuoc Cham Dressing

¼ cup castor sugar

¼ cup fish sauce

¼ cup fresh lime juice

1 fresh red chilli, finely sliced

3 cloves garlic, very finely chopped

Combine all the ingredients in a small jug and stir until the sugar is dissolved.

MAKES ¾ CUP

Gochujang Dressing

5 Tbsp gochujang paste (Korean chilli paste)

3 cloves garlic, minced

2½ Tbsp white sugar

½ green apple, peeled

5 Tbsp rice vinegar

5 Tbsp soya sauce

3 Tbsp sunflower or vegetable oil

2½ Tbsp sesame oil

Fine salt, to taste

5 tsp sesame seeds

Place the gochujang paste, garlic, sugar, apple, rice vinegar, soya sauce and oils in the bowl of a food processor or blender and blend to combine.

Adjust for seasoning, adding more salt, soya sauce, or sweetness as needed. Stir in the sesame seeds.

MAKES 1¾ CUP

Tahini Dressing

½ cup tahini

¼ tsp chilli powder (optional)

¼ tsp za'atar or sumac

½ tsp salt

¼ cup warm water

2 Tbsp freshly squeezed lemon juice

Salt and pepper, to taste

Mix all the ingredients together (stir vigorously!) in a deep jug or bowl, to form a thick sauce. (Use a food processor or immersion blender, if you do not feel inclined to stirring by hand.) Thin down with more warm water if you like, until you have a smooth, creamy dressing. Season with more salt and pepper, to taste.

MAKES 1 CUP

Caesar Wholegrain Mayonnaise

2 Tbsp crushed garlic

8 anchovy fillets

½ cup wholegrain mustard

¼ cup grated parmesan cheese

¼ cup freshly squeezed lemon juice

Zest of 3 lemons, grated

2 cups homemade mayonnaise or Hellman's
    Classic Mayonnaise

½ cup full-cream or Greek yoghurt

Salt and freshly ground black pepper, to taste

In the bowl of a food processor, combine the garlic, anchovies, mustard, parmesan, lemon juice and zest, and process until mixed. Add the mayonnaise and yoghurt and process to combine. Season with salt and black pepper. Store in a sealed, sterilised glass jar. Keeps for 2 weeks.

MAKES 3¼ CUPS (RECIPE CAN BE HALVED)

Poppy Seed Vinaigrette

¼ cup sesame seeds, toasted

1 Tbsp poppy seeds

½ cup white sugar

3 Tbsp minced onion

½ tsp paprika

¼ cup white wine vinegar

¼ cup apple cider vinegar

½ cup sunflower oil

½ tsp salt or fish sauce

In a medium-sized bowl, whisk together all the ingredients until well combined. Store in a sterilised glass jar or bottle in the fridge for up to 6 weeks.

MAKES 2 CUPS

Tonnato Sauce

1 can tuna, drained
¼ tsp salt
½ cup homemade mayonnaise or
   Hellmann's Classic Mayonnaise
¼ cup extra-virgin olive oil
1–2 Tbsp freshly squeezed lemon juice
Zest of 1 lemon, grated (optional)

Blend the tuna and salt in a food processor. Add the mayonnaise and pulse until creamy. With the motor running, drizzle in the olive oil and lemon juice, and blend until the tonnato is exceptionally smooth and creamy.

Adjust for more salt, olive oil or lemon juice and store in an airtight container.

MAKES JUST MORE THAN 1 CUP

Deeply Roasted Sesame Sauce

6 Tbsp white sesame seeds
3 Tbsp Kikkoman soya sauce
2 Tbsp rice wine vinegar
4 tsp mirin
5 tsp honey/agave/brown sugar/moskonfyt
2 tsp sesame oil
2 drops of liquid Maggi seasoning,
   or 4 cloves black garlic (optional)
½ cup Kewpie mayonnaise
6 Tbsp sunflower oil
Salt and freshly ground black pepper,
   to taste

Toast the sesame seeds in a dry pan over medium heat until deeply toasted but not burned. Swirl the seeds in the pan constantly to get an even toasting and prevent burning. Pour the toasted seeds onto a plate or baking tray immediately, to arrest the cooking process.

Pulse the seeds in a food processor, using a spatula to scrape down the sides of the bowl. The mixture should resemble a fine flour but still contain some whole seeds.

Add the soya sauce, vinegar, mirin, desired sweetener, sesame oil, Maggi liquid seasoning (if using) and Kewpie mayonnaise, and blend well. With the motor running, pour in the sunflower oil.

Taste and season with salt and black pepper or more honey, if necessary.

MAKES ± 360 ML

Sumac Dressing

1 clove garlic, crushed

1 tsp salt

1 tsp sweet paprika

2 tsp sumac

4 Tbsp extra-virgin olive oil

2 Tbsp freshly squeezed lemon juice

Whisk all the ingredients together in a jug, or bowl or shake in a jar with a tight lid, until combined.

MAKES ½ CUP

Çemen Paste

This Turkish-inspired paste is wonderful smeared over a lamb shoulder or beef short-ribs before slow roasting with lots of sliced onions for 3 hours (at 180°C). I thin it down to use as a dressing and as a wonderful addition to soups and stews.

1 Tbsp fenugreek seeds, soaked in ± 1½ cm water
    for 10 minutes

3 cloves garlic

3 Tbsp castor sugar

1 tsp salt

3½ Tbsp paprika

1 Tbsp dried chilli flakes

3 Tbsp smoked paprika

2 tsp ground cumin

1 tsp cumin seeds

1 Tbsp chicken or vegetable stock powder

150–200 ml water (you may want to add more to
    make the paste looser, as you prefer)

¼ cup extra-virgin olive oil

Add the soaked fenugreek seeds and garlic to a food processor and purée to a paste. Add all the remaining ingredients and blend again, adding the water and olive oil last. Taste and adjust seasoning with salt or sugar. This paste will keep in an airtight container in the fridge for a good 3 months. You could freeze it too.

MAKES 2 CUPS

3 Spice mixes

Thandai Masala Blend

½ star anise

1 cinnamon stick

5 green cardamom pods (seeds removed)

2 cloves

2 tsp fennel seeds

¼ tsp ground nutmeg

½ tsp black pepper

¼ tsp ground turmeric

Pinch of salt

½ tsp sugar

OPTIONAL ADDITIONS

¼ cup toasted almonds, chopped

1 Tbsp poppy seeds

1 Tbsp rose petals (optional but obviously nice!)

Toast all the spices in a pan over medium heat until fragrant. Remove and add to a spice grinder. Add the salt and sugar and blitz to a fine powder.

Add the toasted almonds and poppy seeds after grinding.

MAKES ¼ CUP

Dukkah Spice Blend

¼ cup coriander seeds

3 tsp fennel seeds

1 tsp dried chilli flakes

1 tsp brown sugar

1 tsp garlic powder

2 tsp salt

Pinch of citric acid

Toast the coriander and fennel seeds, chilli flakes and brown sugar in a dry pan over medium heat until fragrant. Allow to cool, then add the garlic powder, salt and citric acid.

Grind in a spice grinder to a powder, coarse or fine.

MAKES NEARLY ½ CUP

Harissa Spice Blend

2 Tbsp coriander seeds

2 Tbsp cumin seeds

1 Tbsp caraway seeds

1 tsp garlic powder

1 tsp smoked paprika

1 Tbsp dried chilli flakes

1 tsp salt

Toast the coriander, cumin and caraway seeds in a dry pan over medium heat until fragrant. Grind in a spice grinder. Then, in a small bowl, mix the spices with the remaining ingredients.

MAKES NEARLY ½ CUP

[2]

Salads I would have made at The Kitchen

Every few weeks, I would arrive at The Kitchen with an armful of recipes. I'd glean them from a new recipe book or the internet, or they would be an offshoot from the previous night's supper. Sometimes, the recipes would be quite coherent. Sometimes they would take the form of notes: use this technique with this vegetable, take this dressing from that other recipe from a few years back, use that base, finish with these herbs, etc. My team would fall upon these with glee. They would immediately begin adding them to the day's salad menu and make up a little sample plate for me to taste. Oh, how I miss this!

Salads at The Kitchen had to be robust and versatile, and they had to carry a particular flavour or texture. They also had to play nicely with their friends. Only then could they be part of our gang!

Roasted Sweet Potato Salad with Tomato-Tamarind Dressing & Toasted Peanuts

The sourness of the chaat masala comes from amchur, a powder made from dried unripe green mangoes. In this salad, sweet, tart and salty all bounce up against each other, just how I like it! This warm salad can stand centre-stage with a piece of fish or with some green beans on the side.

FOR THE ROASTED SWEET POTATOES

5 large sweet potatoes (preferably orange), scrubbed
½–⅔ cup sunflower oil, for roasting

FOR THE DRESSING

2 tomatoes, diced into ± ½ cm pieces
3 Tbsp tamarind paste
Juice of ½ lemon
1½ tsp chaat masala
1½ Tbsp honey
1 tsp dried chilli flakes
3 Tbsp extra-virgin olive oil

TO SERVE

1 red onion, thinly sliced into rings
½ cup salted peanuts, chopped
20 g fresh coriander, chopped
Flaked sea salt and black pepper, to taste

Preheat the oven to 190°C.

Cut the sweet potatoes into wedges, about 6–8 per potato. In a large bowl, toss the wedges with ½ cup of sunflower oil (or more as needed) until they are evenly coated. Place the wedges on a baking sheet lined with baking paper, pointy sides up, in single file. Roast for 25–35 minutes, until the potatoes are cooked through, soft when squeezed, and slightly brown and caramelised on the edges.

To make the dressing, put the diced tomatoes in a medium bowl together with the tamarind paste, lemon juice, chaat masala, honey, chilli flakes and olive oil. Mix gently until combined. You can also make the dressing without the tomatoes and instead sprinkle them over the sweet potatoes to garnish before serving.

To serve, arrange the roasted sweet potato wedges on a serving platter and spoon over the dressing. Arrange the red onion rings over the salad. Top with the peanuts and fresh coriander, before sprinkling with flaked salt and a brief grinding of black pepper.

SERVES 5–6 AS A SIDE OR 4 AS A MAIN

Broccoli Tonnato with Fried Capers, Rocket & Sunflower Seeds

1 cup sunflower oil

50 g capers

2 heads (± 650 g) broccoli, or 800 g
   long-stemmed broccoli

3 Tbsp extra-virgin olive oil

Juice and grated zest of 1 lemon

Salt and black pepper, to taste

150 g edamame beans or peas (optional)

100 g asparagus (optional)

1–1¼ cups Tonnato Sauce (p. 13)

Maldon salt, to taste

30 g sunflower seeds, toasted

40 g rocket

Heat the oil in a wok over medium-high heat. When hot, deep-fry the capers for about 3 minutes, or until crispy. Remove the crispy capers with a slotted spoon and drain on paper towel.

If using heads of broccoli, cut the heads into florets, using as much stem as you can shape into the floret.

Bring a large pot of water to a boil and blanch the broccoli for 3–5 minutes (and no longer!). Have a large bowl of iced water at the ready. Use a slotted spoon to remove the broccoli florets from the boiling water and place them into their cold bath, thereby arresting the cooking process. Drain the broccoli in a colander. In a large bowl, toss the broccoli with 2 tablespoons of the olive oil and season with a good squeeze of lemon juice, salt and black pepper.

If using, the edamame beans require only a brief submerging, 20 seconds, in the blanching pot, and the asparagus no more than 1 minute. Each green needs an iced water baptism to arrest the cooking process and retain green-ness.

To plate, spread the Tonnato Sauce on a platter or serving plate, leaving a border large enough to frame your dish (and send a message about the delicious sauce beneath the greens). Arrange the broccoli on top of the Tonnato Sauce and layer with the blanched edamame beans and asparagus, if using. Sprinkle the lemon juice and zest over the salad. Drizzle with the remaining olive oil and season with Maldon salt and freshly ground black pepper. Sprinkle the salad with the fried capers and toasted sunflower seeds. Arrange the rocket leaves in a heap on top of the salad so that you can still see all the lovely greens beneath.

**SERVES 6 WITH BROCCOLI ONLY
OR 8 WITH THE OTHER GREENS**

Green Beans with Crispy Garlic, Butter & My Insane Crumbs

Savouring a buttery bean is a solitary pleasure. I would have a bowl of these alone for supper. For a substantial lunch, add an egg! These are a perfect accompaniment for a good piece of fish or a steak, too.

FOR THE BEANS

500 g fine green beans (*see* note below)
¼ cup extra-virgin olive oil
60 g butter
3 cloves garlic, finely sliced

TO SERVE

Flaked sea salt and black pepper
½ cup My Insane Crumbs (p. 173)
½ cup grated parmesan or local hard cheese
  (optional but impressive-looking)

A NOTE ON THE BEANS:

if you cannot find fine green beans, use regular green beans, but slice each one into 3 on a very sharp diagonal (the old people used to do this with a blade).

Top the green beans, keeping their pretty tails. Blanch the beans in a large pot of boiling water for 3–4 minutes. Remove with a slotted spoon or spider spoon and plunge immediately into a bowl of iced water for a minute or two to arrest the cooking process. Drain in a colander.

Add the olive oil and one-third of the butter to a pan. When the butter starts to foam a little, add the garlic and cook, stirring, until golden around the edges. Remove the garlic from the pan with a slotted spoon and transfer to a small plate.

Add the remaining butter to the pan and tip in the drained green beans. Toss them around until they are coated in butter and olive oil. Tip the beans onto a warm serving platter and sprinkle with the golden garlic and My Insane Crumbs. Grate parmesan or hard cheese directly over the top of the beans.

MORE FINE BEAN IDEAS

- Heat Japanese Curry (p. 122) and pour into a serving dish. Add blanched beans and sprinkle liberally with Peanut Chutney Podi (p. 171) and chopped fresh coriander.

- Toss cooked seasoned lentils with Sumac Dressing (p. 14). Pile blanched beans on top of the lentils, drizzle generously with Tahini Dressing (p. 12) and chopped toasted almonds, crispy garlic (as in the recipe above) and chopped fresh parsley.

SERVES 4–6

Kwetsa Pakora & Green Chutney with Chaat Masala

Stoney is a much-loved South African ginger beer. The little burn at the back of your throat (you can get extra now!) is called 'kwetsa'. Why not use Stoney for the sparkly business required for this batter? Chana flour is another one of those ingredients I had lots of when I closed my restaurant. And here is a fun way to use it!

FOR THE GREEN CHUTNEY WITH CHAAT MASALA

5 cm piece fresh ginger, peeled and chopped

1 fresh green chilli, seeds removed, and chopped

1½ cups fresh coriander leaves with tender stems

1½ cups fresh mint leaves

⅓ cup Greek yoghurt

4 tsp freshly squeezed lemon juice

4 tsp vegetable oil

1 tsp chaat masala

Kosher salt, to taste

FOR THE KWETSA PAKORA

1½ cups chana (chickpea) flour

1 tsp ground ginger

½ tsp ground cumin

1 tsp ground coriander

1 tsp mustard seeds

1 tsp garlic powder

½ tsp ground fenugreek (methi) (optional)

½ tsp ground black pepper

½ tsp salt

1 × 330 ml can Stoney Ginger Beer

3 medium eggplants

Sunflower oil, for frying

To make the Green Chutney with Chaat Masala, add all the ingredients to a food processor and pulse until smooth. Season with salt. Store in a jar in the fridge or use straight away.

Make the Kwetsa Pakora batter by whisking the chana flour, ginger, cumin, coriander, mustard seeds, garlic powder, fenugreek, black pepper and salt in a bowl. Slowly add the ginger beer, whisking constantly. Allow the mixture to stand for at least 30 minutes, or even overnight, to allow the flour to hydrate. The batter will become thick and grainy.

Cut the eggplants into wedges (or any shape of your choosing for snacking).

Over medium-high heat, add at least 5 cm of oil to a wok or pan. Stir the batter and dip the eggplant into the batter, allowing the excess to drip back into the bowl. Fry the wedges, 4 or 5 at a time, until they are golden-brown and crispy. Remove the wedges from the pan and drain on paper towel.

Serve with yoghurt topped with a bit of chilli, or any of your favourite relishes from this book. You can also dip the crispy wedges in a bowl of Peanut Chutney Podi (p. 171). I have also dipped whole Swiss chard leaves in this batter, fried them to tremendous effect and served them with tomato soup.

SERVES 6–8 AS A SNACK OR 4 AS A MAIN

Tadka Carrots

This is a perfect recipe, inspired by one in Saliha Mahmood Ahmed's marvellous book, Khazana. She employs the traditional method of frying spices in oil and pouring the hot spiced oil over raw carrots. I am always reaching for the essence of the vegetable. This simple recipe leads us right there, to the soul of the carrot.

500 g carrots, peeled and grated
  (I like to use the grater blade on my food
  processor for this task. It gives a stronger
  grate, which is good for this salad)
5 Tbsp sunflower oil
2 tsp brown mustard seeds
1 heaped Tbsp cumin seeds
½ tsp ground turmeric (or 1 tsp grated
  fresh turmeric)
1 tsp dried chilli flakes
1 cup fresh coriander, leaves and stalks
  finely chopped
Juice of 1 large lemon or of ½ orange
3 Tbsp honey, moskonfyt, or Hot Honey (p. 50)
Salt and a good grinding of black pepper,
  to taste
1 Tbsp Peanut Chutney Podi (p. 171) (optional)

Squeeze out any excess moisture from the grated carrots and place them in a large mixing bowl.

Heat the oil in a pan over medium heat until it is hot but not quite smoking. First, add the mustard seeds and cumin seeds to the hot oil – they will start sizzling and popping immediately. Then, add the turmeric and chilli flakes, stirring quickly for just a few seconds to prevent the spices from burning. Remove from the heat and carefully pour the hot spiced oil over the grated carrots. Make sure to tip the pan away from you as you do so, to avoid burning yourself.

Add the chopped coriander to the carrots, along with the lemon or orange juice, honey, plenty of salt and Peanut Chutney Podi, if using. Toss all the ingredients well and serve the salad at room temperature.

SERVES 4–6

Indian Fried Rice with Lime, Peanuts, Coriander & Chutney Podi

I can eat this rice anytime of the day and night. I love that the lime juice here is treated as a seasoning, and that the nuttiness of the ghee and curry leaves provides comfort. You could add a poached egg on top for a substantial supper. A little tomato sambal or some beetroot pickles would be a delicious addition, too.

3½ cups cooked basmati rice

Juice of 2 limes (± ¼ cup)

Salt, to taste

1 cup roughly chopped fresh coriander

7 Tbsp ghee or butter

1 Tbsp black mustard seeds

A good handful (± 15) fresh curry leaves

1 cup unsalted peanuts (it is not the end of the world if you only have salted peanuts!)

2 small fresh red chillis, halved lengthways and sliced on the diagonal

2 onions, thinly sliced

TO GARNISH

Zest of 1 lime, finely sliced

¼ cup roasted peanuts, chopped

¼ cup roughly chopped fresh coriander

3 Tbsp chutney podi

Add the cooked basmati rice to a large mixing bowl. Season with the lime juice and salt, and toss to combine. Briefly stir through the chopped coriander. Do not overmix the rice at this point; there will be more tossing later.

Heat 4 tablespoons of ghee in a deep pan. Once the ghee begins to shimmer, add the mustard seeds. As soon as they begin to pop, which will happen surprisingly quickly, add the curry leaves and stir until they are well coated in the ghee. The leaves will begin to crisp up (again, surprisingly quickly).

With the pan over low-medium heat, add the peanuts. Cook for 3–5 minutes, stirring continuously, allowing them to turn a medium shade of brown and become fragrant. Pour the peanut-curry-leaf-ghee over the rice and toss briefly and gently to combine. Set aside.

Using the same pan, add the remaining 3 tablespoons of ghee. Once it begins to shimmer, add the chillies and sliced onions, and fry for about 7 minutes, or until they caramelise. Stir the caramelised onions and chillies into the rice until just combined. Do not stir too-too much – the rice should look fresh and bright!

Place the rice in a serving bowl or on a platter. Garnish with the lime zest, roasted peanuts and chopped coriander. Sprinkle the chutney podi liberally over the rice.

SERVES 6

Red Sorghum & Crispy Kale Salad with Chilli Butter, Yoghurt & Hard Cheese

Sorghum is a grain packed with nutrients. It is delicious and nutty and – shhh! – I prefer it to quinoa. Great as a gluten-free alternative to rice and bulgur wheat, in South Africa it is used in the fermented Tswana porridge, ting.

This salad is healthy-ish. The ingredients are without flaw, but the chilli butter is what brings the '-ish' to healthy, adding a rich yumminess to the whole dish.

FOR THE CHILLI BUTTER

185 g salted butter
1 Tbsp harissa paste, or 2 tsp Harissa
    Spice Blend (p. 16), or 1 Tbsp sriracha sauce
Salt and black pepper, to taste

FOR THE CRISPY KALE

250 g kale, central stalks cut out and leaves
    torn into pieces
¼ cup extra-virgin olive oil, divided

FOR THE RED SORGHUM

200 g red sorghum
3 Tbsp sunflower oil
2 onions, halved and finely sliced into
    half moons
5 cloves garlic, thinly sliced
1 cup cranberries, or sliced dried apricots,
    or sultanas
Salt and black pepper, to taste
40 g fresh mint, shredded (with scissors)
40 g fresh Italian parsley, leaves only, shredded

½ cup Greek yoghurt
60 g hard cheese (pecorino, parmesan, or
    very mature cheddar), finely grated

Preheat the oven to 180°C (a fan setting would be perfect).

Make the Chilli Butter by melting together the butter and harissa paste (or chilli element of your choosing). Season to taste, adding more harissa or chilli if you are a chilli-phile.

For the Crispy Kale, line a baking sheet with baking paper. In a large mixing bowl, toss the kale with 2 tablespoons of olive oil to coat. Spread the kale on the baking sheet and roast in the oven for 15 minutes. Turn the sheet every 5 minutes and move the leaves around, if necessary, for an even roast. Leave on a cooling rack to retain crispness.

Bring a generous pot of water to a boil, add the sorghum and cook for 35 minutes, or until tender. (Soak the sorghum overnight to reduce cooking time by 10 minutes). Drain in a colander, rinse briefly with cold water and set aside to cool.

Heat the sunflower oil in a pan, and add the onions and garlic. Sauté gently over low-medium heat, until the onions are translucent and just beginning to colour.

Tip the drained sorghum into a large bowl. Stir in the onions and garlic, as well as the cranberries. Season generously with salt and black pepper. Allow to cool, then add the mint and parsley (to stop the herbs from colouring).

When ready to serve, reheat the Chilli Butter. Spoon the sorghum-onion mixture onto a deep platter or serving plate and dollop the yoghurt over the salad. Arrange the Crispy Kale leaves on top. Pour the Chilli Butter over all (especially the yoghurt) and drizzle with the remaining olive oil. Sprinkle the hard cheese over the salad and serve.

SERVES 6–8 AS A SIDE

Cabbage Tabbouleh

Italian parsley is the star of this green, crunchy tabbouleh. It is as welcome as an oasis!

¼ cup uncooked bulgur wheat

¼ medium head of cabbage (± 4 cups), cored
  and very finely sliced

½ medium white onion, very finely sliced

2 cups finely shredded fresh Italian parsley

½ cup lemon juice

½ cup extra-virgin olive oil

1 tsp ground allspice

Flaked sea salt, to taste

1 cup fresh mint leaves, torn or snipped

½ fresh green chilli, sliced (optional)

Place the bulgur wheat in a medium bowl and cover with about 5 cm of boiling water. Soak for 1 hour, or until tender, then drain in a colander or sieve.

In a large bowl, toss the cooked bulgur wheat with 3 cups of the cabbage, together with the onion and 1 cup of the parsley.

Add the lemon juice, olive oil, allspice and salt, and toss to coat. Finally add the remaining cabbage and parsley, mint and chilli (if using). Give it a final, brief toss before piling on a serving platter.

SERVES 4–6

Beetroot Salad with Cardamom-Ginger-Mint Yoghurt

You might know about my penchant for beetroot salads. People can be concerned about their 'earthiness', but I find them sweet! My rationale is that they are hard to 'beet' on colour (and I'm a colour-blocker of note), and in the evening they do the job that tomatoes do during the day – tomatoes being too fresh and 'cold' at night. Am I being unfair? Bring this one to your palette.

6 medium beetroots
¼ cup extra-virgin olive oil or sunflower oil

FOR THE MINT SAUCE (SEKANJABIN)
½ cup sugar
½ cup water
½ cup fresh mint leaves, shredded,
   plus an extra handful to garnish
2 Tbsp white vinegar

FOR THE YOGHURT DRESSING
½ cup full-cream yoghurt
2 Tbsp apple cider vinegar
1 tsp ground cardamom
5 cm piece fresh ginger, scraped and grated
Salt and black pepper, to taste

TO SERVE
Baby beetroot leaves (from your bunch of
   beetroot), thoroughly washed, to garnish

Cook the beetroot in one of two ways. Drizzle them with the oil and a bit of water, wrap in foil and roast at 180°C for 1½ hours, or until tender. This method delivers a delicious, silky beetroot. Or, boil the beetroots with their skin on for 50 minutes–1 hour, which will deliver the same result. Alternatively, you can cheat and buy them ready cooked! Once the beetroots are cooked and cool enough to handle, slip off their skins and discard. In this recipe, it is the winning dressing that transforms the sliced beetroot into discs of wonder.

Make the Mint Sauce by boiling the sugar and water together, stirring until the sugar dissolves. Let the sugar syrup bubble for 10 minutes, until slightly thickened. Remove from the heat and allow to cool. Once cooled, stir in the shredded mint and white vinegar.

To make the dressing, mix the yoghurt, apple cider vinegar, cardamom, ginger, and some salt and black pepper until well combined.

Slice the roasted beetroots as thinly as you would like and arrange the discs on your prettiest platter. Drizzle over the Yoghurt Dressing and Mint Sauce and layer with more beetroot discs. Finish with a final drizzle of dressing, some shredded mint, the baby beetroot leaves, and salt and black pepper.

NOTE:
This Mint Sauce is wicked with lamb chops, of course, and a very good thing to have in your fridge.

Beetroot Poke with Miso Dressing

Poke bowls originate in Hawaii. They are a mix of fresh ingredients served with raw fish. They are sooo delicious, it is no wonder they have surfed into our world in a big way. This recipe is built around beetroot rather than the freshest fish and, although it is created as a salad for 4 to 6, you could easily plate it up in individual bowls. Do not be alarmed by the list of ingredients. You will find many of them in your fridge.

FOR THE MISO DRESSING

¼ cup miso paste

5 Tbsp Kewpie mayonnaise

1 Tbsp sriracha sauce

1½ Tbsp soya sauce

2 Tbsp honey

2 tsp sesame oil

FOR THE BLACK SUSHI RICE

1 cup black rice

3 cups water

¼ cup rice vinegar

2 tsp vegetable oil

1 tsp salt

2 Tbsp white sugar

FOR THE SALAD BOWL

4 medium beetroot, cooked and skins slipped off

2 avocados, peeled and sliced

½ cup edamame, blanched, or ½ cup baby
   salad leaves

4 spring onions, very finely sliced on the diagonal

2 oranges, peeled and segmented from membrane,
   or 3 persimmons, peeled and very finely sliced

2 carrots, peeled and finely julienned, or ½ cup
   Carrot Daikon Pickle (p. 121)

¼ medium red cabbage, finely julienned

5 radishes, very finely sliced

1 cup Fried Onions (p. 176) or ½ cup shop-bought
   crispy onions

2–3 Soya-Mirin Marinated eggs (p. 126) (optional)

FOR THE TOPPING

Pinch of togarashi

2 Tbsp furikake or gomashio (toasted salt and
   sesame seeds)

To make the Miso Dressing, add all the ingredients to a medium-sized jug and stir to combine. Transfer the dressing to a squeezy bottle, ready for artistic application!

Cook the black rice in the water for 20 minutes, or until tender. Drain the cooked rice in a colander, rinse briefly and allow to cool. While the rice is cooking, make the rice seasoning by combining the rice vinegar, oil, salt and sugar in a small pot. Bring to a boil over medium heat and cook until the sugar dissolves. Allow to cool, then transfer the black rice to a medium mixing bowl and season with the rice-vinegar mix.

Arrange the black rice in a pile in the middle of a platter. Add the salad bowl ingredients in striped 'slopes' down the sides of the rice, arranging as artfully and neatly as you can. Drizzle the whole salad with the Miso Dressing and garnish with togarashi and furikake (or gomashio).

If people feel deprived of Miso Dressing, place the squeezy bottle on the table so they can help themselves.

SERVES 4–6

Chilli Crisp Salad with Celery, Fine Beans, Asparagus, Long-Stemmed Broccoli & Crispy Tofu

The world has been bewitched by Lao Gan Ma Chilli Crisp. And well they may be! It is one of the most powerfully delicious things known to modern humans and can be bought in all Chinese supermarkets. Many have tried to replicate this mythical sauce. My attempt is super delicious (p. 129) and, with its own character, plays wonderfully with the raw vegetables, cut with care by you! Do not balk at the role of celery here. It plays a confident and elegant part in this salad.

120 g green beans, topped but not tailed (optional)

150 g each asparagus and long-stemmed broccoli, tails trimmed

6 celery stalks, trimmed and thinly sliced on a steep diagonal in long, thin half-moons

1 fennel bulb, very finely sliced

200 g tofu, cut into batons or blocks, tossed in rice flour and shallow-fried in sunflower oil

2 Tbsp Gochujang Dressing (p. 10)

Juice of ½ lime

Flaked sea salt, to taste

180 g (about ¾ cup) Walnut Chilli Crisp (p. 129)

¼ cup toasted walnuts, or ½ cup unsalted roasted peanuts, chopped (optional)

7 lively looking celery leaves

Bring a deep pot of water to a boil. Blanch the green beans for 4 minutes. Remove with a slotted spoon and immediately immerse in ice water to arrest the cooking process. Repeat the blanching process with the long-stemmed broccoli for (4 minutes) and the asparagus (1 minute). Cut all the blanched greens on a sharp diagonal, into 6 cm pieces.

Layer the blanched greens, celery and fennel on a platter and distribute the fried tofu on top. Drizzle with the Gochujang Dressing and squeeze over the lime juice. Season with flaked sea salt. Spoon the Walnut Chilli Crisp generously over the salad, along with the toasted walnuts (or peanuts). Garnish with the celery leaves.

SERVES 6

Bhel Puri Potato Salad

This potato salad is flamboyant and fun, with layers of confetti-ed bits vibrant with texture and flavour. You really cannot go wrong. It will bring a smile to your face and delight to others.

4 medium potatoes

¾ cup full-cream yoghurt

5 Tbsp dhanya chutney or similar (I like the Quality Pickles one)

¼ cup freshly squeezed lemon or lime juice

Fine salt and black pepper, to taste

1 cup diced (1 cm pieces) cooked beetroot

1 cucumber, diced into 1 cm pieces

1 fresh red chilli, deseeded and very finely chopped (optional)

1½ red onions, diced into ½ cm pieces

1 cup cubed (1 cm pieces) roasted sweet potato (optional)

80 g dried dates, sliced or chopped

100 g slangetjies (or sev. I like the packets with puffed rice and cornflakes, fennel seeds and other bits. You can buy sev from Indian supermarkets and many corner shops)

100 g plain roasted peanuts (optional but lekker)

Leaves from a bunch of coriander (± 50 g)

Add the potatoes to a large saucepan, cover them with water, bring to a boil and cook for 20–30 minutes, or until tender. Drain and allow to cool before cutting into bite-sized cubes (1½–2 cm). Alternatively, use the Smashed Roasted Potatoes (p. 53) as the base for this potato salad.

In a bowl or deep jug, whisk together the yoghurt, chutney, lemon or lime juice, and season with salt and pepper. Pour this mixture over the potatoes and stir to coat without making mush of your potatoes.

Now begins the exciting layering. Place the potatoes on the base of a serving platter or plate. Next, layer the beetroot, cucumber, chilli (if using), red onions, dates, sweet potatoes (if using), sev, peanuts (if using) and, finally, the coriander leaves. Yay!

SERVES 4–6

[3]

The solace of vegetables

A quieter, slower, more tender aspect to our lives during lockdown brought with it a natural ease towards an even more vegetable-led diet. Meat-centred diets are quite easy: pull out something from your freezer and then add a vegetable or two and there's dinner. When vegetables lead, there is more of a consciousness given to shopping, preparation and planning. Having more time was perfect for this. And, oh, how vegetables brought comfort to our softer spirits! Wholesomeness, purity, gratitude for simplicity. We had everything we needed right here. It was adequate and it was good. There was a graciousness in the way we were living, and a feeling that we were eating well!

Satay Roasted Eggplant

Whenever I make this dish, it is met with rapturous praise. This means that I have made it a number of times, because I am a sucker for applause and affirmation!

4 large eggplants (± 1.2 kg) (*see* note below)

± ¾ cup sunflower oil, divided

4 onions, peeled and finely sliced

3 cloves garlic, peeled and minced

1½ fresh long red chillies, very finely chopped

2 stalks lemongrass, top-third discarded and
   the rest very finely chopped

5 cm piece fresh ginger, peeled and grated

2 Tbsp dark soya sauce

2–3 Tbsp tamarind paste

1 Tbsp soft brown sugar or palm sugar

¾ tsp fine sea salt

250 g crunchy or smooth peanut butter

400 ml water

TO SERVE

Fried onions (shop-bought crispy onions are
   great here, or you can make your own (p. 176)

1 Tbsp chopped peanuts

Fresh herbs – a handful each (80 g in total)
   mint, coriander and dill, all chopped

A NOTE ON THE EGGPLANTS:

I do not salt eggplants. If they are fresh and young, they should be good to go! Generally, I do not peel eggplants either, but if you are worried about a tough roasted skin, do peel the eggplant before slicing it into legs.

Preheat the oven to 200°C and line a baking sheet with baking paper.

Cut each eggplant into an eggplant 'octopus': keeping the top of the eggplant intact, slice down lengthways through the middle, then turn it 90 degrees and slice down lengthways again, to create 4 'legs'. Slice each leg in half, to create 8 legs.

Working over a large bowl, use a brush or your fingers to coat the whole eggplant thoroughly with oil – all over the 8 legs, all the nooks and crannies, and on the outside. Arrange the eggplants head to foot on the baking sheet and roast in the oven for about 30–40 minutes, or until they are soft and beautifully coloured. Check the eggplants 20 minutes into roasting; you might need to give the legs another brush of oil and turn them around to ensure they roast evenly.

While the eggplants are roasting, make the sauce. Heat a quarter cup of oil in a frying pan over medium-low heat and, once it is hot, add the onions, garlic, chillies, lemongrass and ginger. Fry, stirring regularly, for 15–20 minutes, until soft and translucent. Stir in the soya sauce, tamarind paste, sugar, salt and peanut butter, and cook, stirring, for a couple of minutes. Slowly pour in the water, stirring as you go to create a thick sauce.

This dish makes for great individual plating. Create a generous puddle of sauce on a large soup plate or flat-bottomed salad bowl. Nestle the eggplant octopus in the sauce. Scatter over a handful of fried onions, sprinkle with the peanuts and a generous amount of the fresh herbs. Serve with freshly steamed rice and your favourite pickle.

SERVES 4

Fried Radishes on Whipped Feta with Dates, Apples, Red Onion & Radish Tops

The peppery bite of radish, which I often eat with cold butter (it's a great excuse!), is somewhat lost when fried but makes a delightful and pretty vegetable salad with the Whipped Feta. Using the radish tops will make you feel virtuous and stylish!

FOR THE WHIPPED FETA
200 g soft Danish feta
100 ml cream

FOR THE SALAD
1 bunch radishes, well rinsed and dried, preferably with their tops cut off and set aside (or, instead of radish tops, 100 g baby spinach or tender salad leaves)
Sunflower oil, for frying
¼ cup red wine vinegar or your favourite vinaigrette, divided (I love the Poppy Seed Vinaigrette [p. 12] for this salad)
Salt, to taste
Pinch dried chilli flakes
1 Granny Smith or Pink Lady apple, halved, cored, and thinly sliced
½ cup pitted dates, sliced in quarters lengthways
½ red onion, thinly sliced
½ cup toasted almond flakes
20 g Italian parsley, leaves picked
½ tsp sumac
Maldon salt, to taste

To make the Whipped Feta, blend the feta and cream together in a food processor. Set aside.

If you are using radish tops, flash-fry them in a hot, heavy-bottomed frying pan with a few teaspoons of sunflower oil until just wilted. Drizzle with 2 tablespoons of the red wine vinegar or vinaigrette, season with salt, remove from the pan and set aside.

Halve the radishes and heat 2 tablespoons of oil in the same pan. When the oil is shimmering, add the radishes and fry, stirring from time to time, until well-coloured. When they are almost done, at about 5 minutes, add the chilli flakes. Tip the cooked radishes into a bowl and season with the remaining vinegar or vinaigrette. Set aside.

TO ASSEMBLE THE SALAD
Spread the Whipped Feta onto a salad platter. Arrange the fried radish tops over the Whipped Feta. If using baby spinach, spread these leaves over the Whipped Feta, allowing some of the cheese to show beneath the greens. Scatter the fried radishes over the greens. Arrange the sliced apple between the radishes so that they stick up here and there. Scatter the dates and red onion over the salad and sprinkle with the almond flakes and parsley. Dust the whole salad with sumac and add a little Maldon salt.

SERVES 4-6

Poppy Seed Beetroot on Mashed Potatoes with Parsley, Dill & Crispy Potato Skins

Is it wrong to want to colour block one's vegetables? With this combination I feel vindicated, though – the flavours are pure and delicious and the colours exciting. These roots really do want to be companions!

1 kg beetroot, washed and trimmed
    (not peeled; save any leaves that might have
    come with your beetroot)
¼ cup extra-virgin olive oil
1 head garlic, top lopped off, drizzled with oil
    and wrapped in foil
¼ cup Poppy Seed Vinaigrette (p. 12), plus
    extra to drizzle
1 kg potatoes (suitable for mashing), washed,
    peeled, quartered and skins reserved
80 g butter
Salt and white pepper, to taste
175 ml milk, heated
1 cup sunflower oil
Flaked salt, to taste
20 g dill fronds, leaves picked
20 g Italian parsley, leaves picked

In a large pot of water, boil the beetroots for 1 hour, or until soft. After 30 minutes into boiling time, preheat the oven to 200°C. Once the beetroots are cooked, drain them in a colander and, when cool enough to handle, slip off the skins. Use latex gloves to avoid staining your hands. Tear the beetroots into bite-sized chunks, drizzle with olive oil and lay them out on a baking sheet lined with baking paper.

Place the wrapped head of garlic on a separate, small baking sheet. Roast the garlic in the oven for 30 minutes until soft and fragrant, but after 15 minutes, add the beetroots with the garlic. The beetroots will have more colour after roasting but not excitingly so. Tip the roasted beetroot into a medium bowl and toss with the Poppy Seed Vinaigrette. They should now look pleasingly glossy.

When cool enough to handle, squash the soft cloves of garlic out of their skins and set aside on a small saucer.

Meanwhile, boil the potatoes for 15–20 minutes, or until soft. Once cooked, drain in a colander, tip them into a large mixing bowl and add the butter, roasted garlic, and a generous amount of salt and white pepper. Slowly add the hot milk and mash the garlicky potatoes to smooth pillowy-ness. (Do not over mash as this activates the starch in the potatoes and you could end up with an elastic-y mess.)

Heat the sunflower oil in a small pot or wok (keep a slotted spoon handy). Fry the reserved potato skins for 1–3 minutes, or until crispy but not burnt. Transfer to a small bowl and season with salt or your favourite seasoning. Set aside.

Spread the mash on a serving platter. Arrange the glossy beetroot on top. Drizzle with a few more teaspoons of the Poppy Seed Vinaigrette and sprinkle with flaked salt. Spread the dill and parsley leaves over the salad and top with the crispy potato skins.

SERVES 4 AS A MAIN OR 6 AS A SIDE

Roast Pumpkin with Hot Honey & Thandai Citrus Crumbs

Aren't we lucky to be able to take the time to explore all these flavours? The upraised arms of the orange pumpkin wedges invite Hot Honey and the gentle fragrance of the Thandai spice. This roast pumpkin makes for an eye-catching dish and smells wonderful.

FOR THE HOT HONEY

Your favourite honey

Kimchi brine

1 tsp gochujang paste or dried chilli flakes

FOR THE ROAST PUMPKIN

½ pumpkin (± 2 kg)

¼–½ cup sunflower oil

1 tsp salt

½ tsp ground cinnamon

3 Tbsp sugar

2 Tbsp + 1 tsp Thandai Masala Blend (p. 16)

½ cup plain toasted breadcrumbs or panko breadcrumbs (or use My Insane Crumbs recipe without the grated parmesan [p. 173])

Zest of 1 lemon or 1 tsp orange zest

½ tsp flaked sea salt

1 tsp dried rose petals or other small edible petals, to garnish

¼ cup pomegranate jewels (optional), to garnish

To make the Hot Honey, fill a jar two-thirds of the way with honey. Fill the remaining third with kimchi brine. Adjust the proportion of spiciness to sweetness by using less honey and more spicy brine. If you want more heat, add 1 teaspoon of gochujang paste or chilli flakes. There really are no fixed rules for this deliciousness. Pour into a squeezy bottle and set aside for later (you can also drizzle it over anything you can imagine!).

Preheat the oven to 200°C.

Peel and deseed the pumpkin. You will need a strong chef's knife and a good board. Cut the pumpkin into moon-shaped wedges about 4–5 cm thick.

In a large mixing bowl, toss the wedges with the oil, salt, cinnamon and sugar to coat. Lay out the wedges on a baking sheet lined with baking paper and roast for 30–40 minutes. Turn the wedges and the baking tray halfway through, at about 20 minutes, and sprinkle with 1 tablespoon of the Thandai Masala Blend. The pumpkin should be very tender, evenly roasted and caramelised on the edges. Pinch a wedge gently with your fingers to test. No one wants undercooked pumpkin!

Combine the toasted breadcrumbs, lemon (or orange) zest, the remaining Thandai Masala Blend, and the flaked salt in a small bowl.

Using a large fish slice, transfer the pumpkin wedges to a large platter. Drizzle over the Hot Honey, sprinkle the Thandai breadcrumbs on the edges of the wedges and garnish with petals and the pomegranate jewels (if using).

SERVES 6–8

Leigh's Kale Salad
with Garlic, Parmesan & Almonds

I have made many kale salads but this one is my default. My friend Leigh offered it to me after I hauled a very large bunch of kale from her garden (along with other vegetable treasures). It is by far my favourite and crazily addictive!

1 large bunch (± 6 cups) kale
1 clove garlic, finely grated
Juice of ½–1 lemon
¼ cup extra-virgin olive oil
½ tsp salt
Freshly ground black pepper, to taste
½ cup almonds, toasted and quite
   finely chopped
¼ cup grated parmesan cheese

Wash the kale thoroughly, spin dry in a salad spinner, then cut the ribs from the leaves. Shred the leaves finely and add them to a large mixing bowl.

Make the dressing by combining the garlic, lemon juice and olive oil, and season with salt and black pepper. Pour the dressing over the leaves and add the almonds and grated parmesan. Toss very well to coat. Check for seasoning and add more salt and black pepper to taste.

This salad can stand for a good few hours or even overnight in the fridge.

SERVES 4–6

Smashed Roasted Potatoes with a Few Suggestions

How can something so good (I'll take a potato any way I can!) be a 'deadly nightshade'? Certainly potatoes throw shade on lofty (above the ground) vegetables, being so versatile and favoured by modern humans. Somehow, in the collective mind of my family, the presence of a roasted potato in a meal somehow makes it a legit!

1 kg baby potatoes
½ cup sunflower oil
Fine salt or grill seasoning, to taste
Flaked sea salt and freshly ground
   black pepper, to taste

Boil the baby potatoes skin-on in plenty of well-salted boiling water for 20–25 minutes, or until tender.

Meanwhile, preheat the oven to 220°C. When the potatoes have 5 minutes to go until done, place a baking sheet in the oven to heat. Have another baking sheet ready as your squashing tool.

Drain the cooked potatoes in a colander. Remove the hot baking sheet from the oven. Toss all the potatoes onto the baking sheet and immediately use your squasher sheet to press down on the poor, unsuspecting baby potatoes. Now, working quickly, drizzle the sunflower oil over the squashed potatoes, turning them in the oil with a spatula, if necessary, to coat. Sprinkle the potatoes generously with salt or your favourite grill seasoning.

Return the sheet with your seasoned potatoes to the oven quick-quick and blast roast for 20–30 minutes, until golden and crispy.

Slide the potatoes onto a large, generous platter and season generously with flaked sea salt and freshly ground black pepper.

SERVES 4 – JUST ABOUT!

OPTIONS FOR TOPPINGS
- *Tonnato Sauce (p. 13) with white beans, boiled eggs, capers and a pile of shredded lettuce.*
- *Garlicky yoghurt drizzled with harissa and topped with blanched fine greens like asparagus, long-stemmed broccoli and peas.*
- *Whipped Feta (p. 46), roughly chopped tomatoes, finely shredded spinach and Fried Onions (p. 176).*
- *Miso Dressing (p. 36), finely shaved fennel, carrot, and radish, a few cranberries and coriander leaves.*

Melting Caramelised Cabbage with Ginger-Fennel Smoor

This is a hug of a dish. Sometimes we need a reassuring dish to let us know that everything is going to be OK – different to what we might have planned – and that there are sunrises and sunsets, sometimes aching hearts and grief but also bowls of melting cabbage for comfort and restoration. This smoor is a great one to have in your arsenal.

FOR THE GINGER-FENNEL SMOOR

2 medium onions, chopped

3 cloves garlic, minced

3 cm piece fresh ginger, minced

¼ cup extra-virgin olive oil

1 tsp ground coriander

1 tsp ground cumin

1 tsp fennel seeds

½ tsp dried chilli flakes

¼ cup tomato paste

5 ripe tomatoes (preferably plum), diced,
   or 1 can diced tomatoes

2 Tbsp soya sauce

1 Tbsp sugar or honey

3 Tbsp ouzo (optional)

½ cup water

1 tsp salt and white pepper, to taste

FOR THE CARAMELISED CABBAGE

3 Tbsp vegetable oil

1 medium cabbage, sliced into 8 wedges with
   the core intact (it keeps the wedges together)

½ cup water

2 Tbsp extra-virgin olive oil

Salt and black pepper, to taste

TO SERVE

½ cup Greek yoghurt

A few sprigs of fresh dill, picked

Harissa or sriracha sauce (optional), to taste

To make the Ginger-Fennel Smoor, fry the onions, garlic and ginger in the olive oil over medium-high heat for 8–10 minutes, until the onions are translucent. Add the coriander, cumin, fennel seeds and chilli flakes, and fry for another 5 minutes, stirring regularly. Add the tomato paste, tomatoes, soya sauce, sugar, ouzo (if using), salt and white pepper. Let the sauce bubble away for another 15 minutes over low heat until it thickens slightly. Pour the tomato sauce into a baking dish (preferably one with a lid) that you will use for the caramelised cabbage wedges.

Preheat the oven to 180°C.

To make the Caramelised Cabbage, heat the vegetable oil in a large pan and fry the cabbage wedges, cut-side down, over high heat for 3–5 minutes on each side, until they caramelise on the edges. You will need good tongs to turn them. Place the caramelised wedges in the baking dish on top of the tomato sauce. If the wedges have disintegrated slightly while frying, use your tongs to piece them together into your baking dish. When all are done, pour the water around the cabbage wedges and drizzle with the olive oil. Season the cabbage wedges with salt and black pepper.

Put the lid on the dish or cover tightly with foil and bake for 30 minutes. Then, remove the cover and bake uncovered for a further 10–15 minutes. The cabbage will be incredibly soft and yielding. Serve with yoghurt, dill, and harissa or sriracha, if you are so inclined.

SERVES 4–6

Gems Lamarque

From the moment Ingrid Lamarque set foot on South African soil, she longed with a great European yearning for wide, hot, open, barren desert space with big blue skies. She came to stay with me in my Zeekoevlei bungalow. Finally, I was forced to take her on a road trip to satisfy this urgent dream. I thought the Karoo would do it: hot, dry, vast open space. No. Ingrid wanted more barrenness. Our road trip would eventually take us to the Kalahari (Ingrid happier) and Namibia (Ingrid smiling), an expansive 5050 km, my little tent pitched under African skies.

When I went to visit Ingrid in France it was in the depths of winter and I wanted cold butter, good bread and cheese, and rural cooking. What a wonderful feast of a time I had, bouncing across the French countryside in Ingrid's TGV à toute vitesse with her (quite wild) friends! In a short time, I learned a lot about the way the French eat. And I will never forget this wondrous and deceptive sauce au poivre vert... But I have named it after these memories.

4 gem lettuce heads, small to medium-sized

1½ Tbsp extra-virgin olive oil

2 tsp peppercorn brine

¾ cup fresh cream

3 tsp brined green peppercorns, squashed
   with the flat of a cook's knife

1 Tbsp vegetable or chicken stock powder

80 g frozen garden peas or petit pois, defrosted

1 spring onion, sliced

Flaked sea salt and freshly ground black pepper,
   to taste

Cut each lettuce head in half lengthways. Add the olive oil to a wide pan and, once hot, add 4 gem lettuce halves to the pan, cut-side down. With a wide spatula or a lid, press down on the gems to create a sear. Move the lettuce around the pan to pick up some oil to aid the sear. This should take no more than 4–5 minutes. Turn the gems over to give the other side some colour and to allow them to collapse a little, for another 1–2 minutes. Transfer the cooked lettuces to a serving platter and drizzle with the peppercorn brine. Repeat this method with the remaining 4 lettuce halves. Once done, wipe out the pan with paper towel.

To make the Lamarque sauce, add the cream to the cleaned pan and heat it until it begins to bubble. Add the squashed peppercorns and swirl these through the cream. Stir in the stock powder and allow the sauce to simmer gently for 3–4 minutes. It should reduce and thicken. Add half the peas to the cream mixture.

Pour the Lamarque sauce over the seared gems. Sprinkle with the sliced spring onion and the remaining peas. Finish with flaked salt and freshly ground black pepper.

SERVES 4

NOTE:
This sauce is also lovely with blanched baby onions, other greens, steak, fish and chicken.

Parsnip & Apple Purée with Fatty Crispy Puffed Rice

I love purée but I know it is very divisive ('it's baby food, Karen!'). So, in my home, it is a bit of a private indulgence. But with the Fatty Crispy Rice it becomes an altogether more adult experience. You could thin down the purée with water or stock to make a soup and give it the same crispy topping treatment. Serve both purée or soup in small bowls or cups.

500 g parsnips, peeled and chopped
1 green apple, peeled and chopped
2 tsp vegetable or chicken stock powder
120 ml cream
Salt and white pepper, to taste
1 cup Fatty Crispy Puffed Rice (p. 176)
10 g finely chopped parsley or 1 spring onion, finely sliced (optional)

Boil the parsnips and apple in water for 20–25 minutes, or until soft. Drain the cooked parsnips and apple and reserve 150–180 ml of the water. Place the cooked parsnip and apple pieces in a food processor (or use an immersion blender in a big jug). Add the stock powder and purée and, with the motor running, add the reserved water. Drizzle in the cream in this way too. Taste and adjust for seasoning.

Serve with a generous amount of Fatty Crispy Rice piled on top. Garnish with parsley or spring onion, if you prefer.

SERVES 4

[4]

My brassica affair

You will find in this book a definite leaning towards broccoli, cauliflower, Brussels sprouts and a cruciferous cabbage, too. Forgive me, sweet pepper and butternut lovers. I confess this affair for what it is: lusty, playfully experimental, selfish and brazen!

Sesame-Cured Broccoli Salad

Melissa Clark's recipe for this broccoli salad had me intrigued, because, boy, do I have a slew of broccoli salads in my repertoire! I have been seduced by this method of 'curing' the raw broccoli to a bright green with the vinegar and then the oil. I could eat the whole bowl!

2 tsp red wine vinegar

1 tsp Maldon salt, plus more to taste

Florets from 2 heads broccoli, sliced as
    thinly as possible

¾ cup extra-virgin olive oil

4 fat cloves garlic, minced

2 tsp cumin seeds

2 tsp sesame oil

Large pinch of dried chilli flakes

Salt and freshly ground black pepper, to taste

In a large heatproof bowl, stir together the vinegar and salt. Add the sliced broccoli florets and toss to combine.

In a pan set over medium-high heat, heat the olive oil. Add the garlic and cumin seeds, and cook for about 1 minute, stirring constantly, until fragrant. Do not let the garlic burn. If necessary, remove the pan from the heat and let the garlic and cumin cook in the residual heat of the oil.

Stir in the sesame oil and chilli flakes, and pour the mixture over the broccoli. Toss well to coat.

Allow the salad to sit for at least an hour at room temperature for the flavours to develop and the broccoli to 'cure' in the flavoured oil. The salad can be refrigerated for up to 48 hours. Before serving, taste and adjust the seasoning, if needed. This is a salad that should be served at room temperature.

SERVES 6–8

Brussels Sprouts with Nuoc Cham Dressing

I did not grow up with Brussels sprouts and so know little about the soggy smell of overcooked Brussels sprouts that have ruined this vegetable for so many. No Brussels sprout in my home has ever seen water. I adore Brussels sprouts! Roasted or 'popcorned', they are a vegetable canvas, inviting almost any dressing, butter, cream or topping – and they are quirky friends to other vegetables.

2 Tbsp vegetable oil

300 g Brussels sprouts, washed and halved vertically through the core

¼ cup Nuoc Cham Dressing (p. 10)

20 g butter (about 2 pats)

Drizzle of Hot Honey (p. 50) (optional)

2 Tbsp toasted black sesame seeds

20 g fresh mint, snipped, or fresh coriander, roughly chopped

OPTIONAL TOPPINGS

100 g roasted peanuts, roughly chopped

20 g bean sprouts

3 spring onions, finely sliced on a sharp diagonal

Heat the oil in a wide, heavy-bottomed pan. Add the Brussels sprouts to a satisfying 'tsssss'.

Fry the sprouts for 4–5 minutes, allowing them to get plenty of colour on one side, then stir and continue frying for another 3–4 minutes so that they colour on the other sides too. When you are satisfied that the Brussels sprouts are mostly cooked, splash the Nuoc Cham Dressing into the pan and shake for about 30 seconds to coat the sprouts. Add the butter pat by pat to the hot pan, stirring and shaking the pan all the while.

Pour the Brussels sprouts with all the sauce into a deep platter. Drizzle with Hot Honey (if using), sprinkle with the toasted black sesame seeds, and fresh mint and coriander. Top with any or all of the optional toppings for a south-east Asian flourish.

SERVES 5–6

Warm Broccoli Spoon Salad

This is an arresting salad, bursting with excellent flavours and so very easy to make. It can stand for a while, too, if you wish to prepare it ahead of time. As the name suggests, it should be eaten from a bowl with a spoon – a much kinder utensil.

¼ cup sunflower oil

1 tsp minced garlic

1½ tsp garam masala (or curry powder, ras el hanout, or similar)

1 tsp chaat masala

1½ Tbsp honey or jaggery (*see* note below)

3 Tbsp freshly squeezed lemon juice

2 Tbsp white wine vinegar

¼ cup toasted almonds, chopped

⅓ cup chopped pitted dates

1 large head broccoli, stems peeled and finely sliced or chopped (I steam mine for 2 minutes in the microwave to add colour)

Salt and black pepper, to taste

½ cup chopped fresh Italian parsley, to garnish (optional)

Heat the oil in a small pan over medium heat. Add the garlic, garam masala and chaat masala, and cook for 2 minutes, stirring constantly. Remove from the heat and add the honey (or jaggery), lemon juice, vinegar, almonds and dates. Stir well to combine.

Pour the hot mixture over the raw (or briefly steamed) broccoli and toss to coat.

Season with salt and black pepper, and garnish with a little extra parsley if you have.

Serve immediately.

SERVES 3–4

NOTE:

Jaggery is a soft cane and palm sugar that originates on the Indian subcontinent. It has a rich caramel flavour. If you can't find it in Indian or Cape Malay shops, substitute with coconut sugar.

Crispy Gochujang Cauliflower

There is a reason for the growing fervour for Korean food outside of Korea. These flavours are insanely good and prick our curiosity – comforting and interesting all at the same time. This cauliflower answers to crisp, manageably spicy and sweet umami. Of course, you are going to love it!

80 g all-purpose flour
80 g cornflour or rice flour
1½ Tbsp cold water
1 large cauliflower (± 500 g), cut into florets
60 g panko breadcrumbs
Vegetable oil, for roasting
1 cup Gochujang Dressing (p. 10)
1 Tbsp toasted sesame seeds, to garnish
2 spring onions, finely sliced, to garnish

Preheat the oven to 190°C.

Make a thin batter by whisking together the flours and water. Dip the cauliflower florets in the batter and then in the breadcrumbs. Line up the crumbed florets on a baking sheet lined with baking paper.

Spray or drizzle vegetable oil over the crumbed florets and bake for 20–30 minutes, until well coloured and crispy. At 15 minutes, you can turn them and re-oil, if necessary, for a more even crispiness.

When the cauliflower has finished roasting, prepare to coat each floret in the dressing. Place three-quarters of the dressing in a smaller, deeper bowl. Use tongs to baptise each floret in the dressing before piling them onto a plate or in bowls. Use the remaining dressing for a final drizzle of goodness.

Garnish with toasted sesame seeds and finely sliced spring onions.

These are an irresistible snack or can be a fine supper with rice. Greens or pickles on the side are always a good idea.

SERVES 3–4

Cauliflower Barley Cheat Risotto with a Gremolata Topping

I believe in cooking in deeper, larger pots so that one can stir with impunity! And I love a big wooden spoon (street traders often have great ones!). Risotto, even a cheat one such as this, requires a lot of stirring and visual engagement.

Sometimes we can spend a lot of time 'making do', hoping that something better will come along. Before we know it, time has passed us by and our quiet disgruntlement and frustration/martyrdom has got us nowhere. Demand the right stuff, even from yourself. Go and buy that microplane/salad spinner/vegetable peeler. Gather the tools to have fun and get the job done!

FOR THE GREMOLATA TOPPING

¼ cup parsley leaves, finely chopped (save the stalks for the risotto)

2 spring onions, finely chopped

1 clove garlic, finely grated

Zest of 1 lemon

FOR THE CHEAT RISOTTO

¼ cup vegetable oil

1 onion, diced

3 leeks, washed and sliced

3 cloves garlic, minced

½ cup parsley stalks or 1 stick celery, diced

1½ heads cauliflower, chopped

Salt and white pepper, to taste

3 cups hot chicken stock

3 cups cooked barley

60 g butter, cut into 3 or 4 pats

¼ cup grated parmesan cheese, or any other hard cheese

120 g mature cheddar, grated, to garnish

To make the Gremolata Topping, combine all the ingredients in a medium-sized bowl and stir to combine.

To make the risotto, place a large, heavy-bottomed pot over medium heat. Heat the oil, and add the onion and leeks. Cook for 8–10 minutes, until the onion is translucent. Add the garlic, parsley stalks and cauliflower, and season with salt and white pepper. Cook for a further 8 minutes, stirring, allowing all the flavours to become acquainted.

Have your hot stock at hand. Add the cooked barley to the pot, turn up the heat and stir constantly for another 3 minutes. Now, begin adding the stock, half a cup at a time, to the 'thirsty' barley risotto, stirring all the while, adding stock until the mixture is creamy. Stir in the butter and the parmesan cheese.

To serve, spoon the risotto into bowls, top with the grated cheddar and then with the fresh gremolata.

SERVES 4–6

Red Cabbage with Capers, Basil & Pine Nuts

I have a childhood memory of cracking pine nuts (dennepitte) with a stone in a pine forest. Such painstaking work for children! Such precious reaping! No wonder pine nuts are dear. They do go rancid quite quickly, though, so don't hold out too long for that special occasion to use them. Set those gold nuggets in this jewel-toned salad.

½ cup pine nuts
1 medium head red cabbage
¼ cup extra-virgin olive oil
1 red onion, thinly sliced
Juice of 1 lemon
3 Tbsp vinaigrette of your choice
1½ Tbsp capers
Salt and black pepper, to taste
100 g soft Danish feta or chevre
1 Tbsp Hot Honey (p. 48), to finish (optional)
15 basil leaves, torn

Toast the pine nuts in a dry pan, shaking or stirring constantly to prevent burning. When they release their aroma, remove from the heat immediately and tip onto a plate to cool.

Cut the cabbage into quarters and slice each quarter very finely into thin strips. Discard the ribs into your compost bucket.

Heat the olive oil in a large, heavy-bottomed pan over medium-high heat. Add the red onion and fry for 3 minutes, stirring constantly. Then, add the sliced cabbage and toss quickly in the heat for about 2 minutes, until it starts to wilt but is still crunchy. Add the lemon juice, vinaigrette and capers, and toss until evenly mixed. Remove from the heat and season with salt and black pepper.

Tip the salad onto a serving platter. Break up the feta into chunks with your fingers and dot all over the cabbage. Drizzle over the Hot Honey, if using. Sprinkle with the toasted pine nuts and garnish with the basil leaves. Serve warm.

SERVES 4

Caramelised Cabbage Wedges with Buttermilk Dressing, Chives & Fatty Crispy Puffed Rice

I have had some champion American wedge salads in my time. I do LOVE an iceberg lettuce, slick with dressing, fresh and crunchy! Cabbage has a similar structure. I find a silky roasted cabbage very appealing in its humble conviviality and willingness to be friends with so many other dishes. I love how handsome it looks, too, with all its wavy leaves a little sizzled on the edges. So, here is the notion of the wedge salad applied to our fetching friend, the cabbage. I have used the irresistible Fatty Crispy Puffed Rice (p. 176) to finish off this dish, but you could substitute with the traditional crumbled blue cheese, parmesan, or even some croutons or My Insane Crumbs (p. 173). Chives are imperative.

FOR THE CARAMELISED CABBAGE

1 medium cabbage
¼ cup olive oil
Pinch of sea salt

FOR THE BUTTERMILK DRESSING

½ cup buttermilk
⅓ cup full-cream or Greek yoghurt
¼ cup homemade mayonnaise or Hellmann's
    Classic Mayonnaise
2 Tbsp freshly squeezed lemon juice
1 Tbsp snipped chives
Salt, to taste

TO FINISH

Finely grated zest of ½ lemon
2 Tbsp snipped chives
Flaked sea salt and freshly ground black pepper,
    to taste
½ cup Fatty Crispy Puffed Rice (p. 176)

Preheat the oven to 200°C.

Cut the cabbage into 8 wedges. Line a baking sheet with baking paper. Pour the olive oil onto the paper and, one by one, baptise the wedges in this pool, ensuring that each wedge is coated well in the oil. Sprinkle lightly with salt. Roast the cabbage in the oven, uncovered, for 15–20 minutes, until it is tender-crisp and has slightly charred bits. Keep an eye on the wedges and turn them halfway through to ensure the cabbage colours evenly.

While the wedges are roasting, make the Buttermilk Dressing by combining all the dressing ingredients in a medium-sized jug.

When the wedges are cooked through, carefully lift them onto your chosen platter using a large, flat spatula or fish slice. Drizzle generously with the Buttermilk Dressing, sprinkle over the lemon zest and chives, and season with salt and freshly ground black pepper. Finish with a sprinkling of Fatty Crispy Puffed Rice.

SERVES 4–6

[5]

Actual lunch and supper

My children grew up with a mom who cooked food for other people. She came home after a long day, smelling of that heady mix of perfume and cooked food. Making supper required a supernatural effort. Chopping an onion or a clove of garlic was an act of loving devotion. It is not that my family ate badly. Hurriedly prepared meals, yes. Shortcuts, yes. Leftovers, yes. Little by way of homemade treats and cake.

The best reward to come from my change of pace after closing The Kitchen was the joy of cooking for my family. Just for them. Not out of obligation or with hurried urgency but by channelling the full power of my creativity and energy, normally spent on others, towards them entirely. The simplicity of this realisation brought into focus the cost of my devotion to others. I understand now their gracious acceptance and their patience with me, a gruff sergeant major. I think the very act of making *actual* lunch for my family has initiated in me a growth towards a transformed, more patient and loving mom.

Five-Spice Chicken & Pork Meatballs with Deeply Roasted Sesame Sauce

These humble ingredients are transformed into unctuous fragrant balls that are 'the bomb', according to my family. They make fantastic snacks and leftovers are terrific on sandwiches the next day with a little Fennel Jam (p. 128).

FOR THE MEATBALLS

600 g boneless chicken thighs

400 g pork mince (or mince from 400 g pork bangers)

3 Tbsp grated ginger

1½ Tbsp sesame oil

2 Tbsp fish sauce

2 spring onions, very finely chopped

½ fresh green chilli, very finely diced (optional)

2 tsp white pepper

¼ tsp Chinese five-spice powder

Sunflower oil, for shaping the balls

TO SERVE

1½ cups Deeply Roasted Sesame Sauce (p. 13)

½ cup Walnut Chilli Crisp (p. 129) or Lao Gun Ma Chilli Crisp

2 Tbsp toasted black sesame seeds mixed with a pinch of Chinese five-spice powder

2 Tbsp finely snipped chives

Cut the chicken thighs into 2 cm chunks. Lay out these chunks on a baking tray and place in the freezer for 1 hour until hardened.

Preheat your oven to the grill + fan setting on high. Line a baking sheet with baking paper.

Transfer the hardened chicken thighs to a food processor and pulse a few times until the chicken is coarsely ground into about ½ cm pieces. Add the pork mince, ginger, sesame oil, fish sauce, spring onions, chilli (if using), white pepper and Chinese five-spice, and mix with the coarse chicken 'mince'. Continue to blitz the mixture in the food processor, stopping regularly to scrape down the sides, until the ingredients are well combined and all the seasonings are distributed through the mince.

Rub your hands with the sunflower oil and shape the mince mixture into 20 (or more) golf ball-sized balls. Lay them on the lined baking sheet. Grill-bake the balls for 11–13 minutes, turning them gently halfway through with a pair of tongs or a palette knife, so they are beautifully tanned all over.

To serve, lay the meatballs on a platter. Pour the Deeply Roasted Sesame Sauce all over the balls and spoon over the Walnut Chilli Crisp. Sprinkle with black sesame seeds (if using) and the snipped chives.

MAKES ± 20 MEATBALLS
SERVES 6 AS A MAIN OR 8 OR MORE AS A SNACK

'Smoked' Basil Chicken Thighs

Who doesn't love the flavour of chicken cooked over fire? It has taken Saliha Mahmood Ahmed to teach me this Mughal cooking technique, dhuandar: a way to impart the flavour of smoke into cooked chicken without fire! My friends in Durban have been doing this for generations. Ah, I have so much to learn!

**FOR THE CHICKEN MARINADE
(OR USE 1 CUP GREEN CHUTNEY
WITH CHAAT MASALA [P. 26])**

100 g Greek yoghurt

3 tsp grated ginger

1 clove garlic, finely grated

30 g fresh basil leaves, divided

1 Tbsp garam masala

1 Tbsp dried chilli flakes

1 Tbsp cumin seeds

½ tsp salt

FOR THE SMOKED CHICKEN

800 g boneless chicken thighs (*see note*)

1 small piece of coal, about 4 × 4 cm

Vegetable oil, for grilling, + 1 Tbsp

NOTE:

I love smoky chicken skin, so I usually debone the thighs myself just so I can get some skin. Skinless thighs are readily available at the supermarket and work well, too.

To make the marinade, add the yoghurt, ginger, garlic, half the basil leaves, garam masala, chilli flakes, cumin seeds and salt to a food processor. Blitz until you have a smooth green purée. Alternatively, use 1 cup of Green Chutney with Chaat Masala (p. 26).

Place the chicken thighs in a glass or casserole dish. Pour your chosen marinade over them. Cover with cling wrap and allow the chicken to marinate for 30 minutes. If you are marinating the chicken for longer than 30 minutes, store it in the fridge.

Preheat the oven to 220°C.

Take a piece of coal and, using kitchen tongs, hold it directly over a gas flame. Getting the coal glowing takes longer than you might think, so get this process going a good 15–20 minutes before you plan to use it.

Place a griddle pan over high heat and brush it lightly with vegetable oil. When it is super-hot, grill the marinated chicken thighs for 5–7 minutes on each side, until cooked through. Place the cooked chicken in a casserole dish with a lid or a heavy cast-iron pot with a lid.

Here is the fun bit: put a large metal serving spoon into the casserole dish on top of the cooked chicken and place the glowing coal on the spoon. Working quickly, pour the oil onto the piece of coal. Smoke will form immediately! Quickly replace the lid of the casserole (no peeking!) and allow the smoke to infuse the chicken for about 15–20 minutes (the pot need not be on the heat).

Serve with a tamarind or garam masala raita and a lovely salad. Top with the remaining basil leaves. This is great served with Beetroot Salad with Cardamom-Ginger-Mint Yoghurt (p. 35).

SERVES 6

Millet Cakes with Turmeric, Feta & Cranberries

In terms of texture and flavour, I would position these moreish millet cakes between the rice-y crunch of Persian scorched tahdig *rice and an Indian fried* dahi *toast. The feta and yoghurt make these cakes creamy on the inside but it is the crunch, always the crunch (!), that makes you want to reach for more!*

¾ cup uncooked millet + 2 cups water for cooking the millet (or 2½ cups cooked millet)

Pinch of salt

1½ tsp grated fresh turmeric

¼ cup red onion, finely diced

55 g dried cranberries, roughly chopped if large

2 tsp black mustard seeds

1 tsp sugar

1 fresh green chilli, finely chopped

½ tsp freshly ground black pepper (this activates the turmeric and is a great friend of feta)

120 g full-cream yoghurt

1 Tbsp cornflour (optional)

2 eggs, lightly beaten

120 g feta, broken into chunks

2 Tbsp fresh curry leaves

½ cup sunflower oil or ghee

If using uncooked millet, dry-toast it in a medium-sized saucepan for 3–4 minutes, stirring constantly. Add the water and a pinch of salt to the toasted millet and bring to a boil over high heat. Once it begins to boil, cover the saucepan, lower the heat and cook gently for 17 minutes, or until done. The grains of millet will look slightly bigger than couscous but with the same 'dry' texture. Set aside to cool before using.

For the millet cakes, stir together the turmeric, red onion, cranberries, mustard seeds, sugar, green chilli, black pepper, yoghurt, cornflour (if using) and beaten eggs. Add the cooked millet, fold in the feta, and leave to rest for 10 minutes.

Shape the millet mixture into small patties just smaller than a ¼ cup measure and about 1½ cm high. The mixture will be wet but should hold together when squashed. I press a curry leaf onto each cake just as I am about to fry it. Use half the leaves for this.

Heat half the oil (or ghee) in a pan set over medium-high heat. Fry the cakes until properly toasted and crisp on the outside, about 3 minutes on each side. Add the remaining curry leaves to the oil in the pan when the cakes have nearly finished cooking (they will have 30 seconds or so in the hot oil). Some millet will spatter and *spat* initially with the first few cakes. Once they are deeply coloured and crisp, remove the cakes to a plate lined with paper towel. Add the remaining oil or ghee to the pan and continue frying until you have used all the mixture.

Serve the millet cakes hot and crispy (they warm up well in an air fryer) with sriracha sauce, Green Chutney with Chaat Masala (p. 26), or your favourite chutney or tomato sauce.

MAKES 12 CAKES

Pasta with a lot of Onions, Crispy Chickpeas & Gremolata Pesto

When I yielded to the idea of using my food processor to slice onions, an entire world of possibility revealed itself! I had until recently been quite pedantic about manual slicing. As much as I worship onions as the basis of all food with soul, the thought of coming home, the smell of kitchen still clinging to my clothes, and having to chop an onion and peel garlic felt like an act of sacrificial devotion. In this recipe, you cook the onions through translucence into caramelly sweetness – the classic Maillard effect. For this pasta, you do need a lot of onions, since they reduce to this allium transfiguration! Add salt, put the lid on and allow for a bit of sweating and confit-ing. Then turn up the heat and take them to perfect flavour.

FOR THE GREMOLATA PESTO

One bunch (± 80 g) curly parsley, soaked, washed and spun dry in a salad spinner
One clove garlic, grated
Zest 1 lemon and juice of 1½
¼ cup olive oil
½ cup sunflower oil
Salt and black pepper, to taste

FOR THE ONIONS

¼ cup sunflower oil
6 onions, halved lengthways and finely sliced into half-moons
1 tsp salt

500 g bowtie (farfalle) pasta or similar
1 pat butter (± 20 g)
Maldon salt and freshly ground black pepper, to taste
1 tsp za'atar
⅔ cup Crispy Roasted Chickpeas (p. 177)

To make the Gremolata Pesto, place the parsley, garlic and lemon zest in the bowl of a food processor. With the motor running, add the lemon juice and then slowly drizzle in the oils to make a pesto. Season with salt and black pepper. For this recipe, add 2 tablespoons of water and more lemon juice to create a looser dressing which can be drizzled. Set aside.

To make the onions, heat the sunflower oil in a deep pot over medium-high heat. Once hot, add all the sliced onions and the salt. Stir briefly to coat the onions in the oil, then leave to cook over medium heat for 20–30 minutes, stirring every 8 minutes or so. Once the onions begin to colour, turn up the heat and cook for another 12–15 minutes, stirring every 3 minutes, until the onions caramelise.

Bring a large pot of water to a boil, salt generously and boil the pasta until al dente. Place the cooked pasta in a large mixing bowl with a pat of butter. Add the caramelised onions, Maldon salt, a good grinding of black pepper, the za'tar and all the crispy chickpeas. Drizzle over ¼–½ cup of the Gremolata Pesto and serve!

SERVES 4–6

'Moroccan' Smoor with a Ginger-Turmeric Yoghurt

This smoor carries two of my favourite flavours in its mirepoix: star anise and cinnamon. And, to finish off, a Ginger-Turmeric Yoghurt. It is seriously delicious and quick-quick to make! Loaded with chickpeas, Israeli couscous and dates, you will want to add this one to your arsenal. You'll find it endlessly useful to use as a sauce, a base or as a soup.

FOR THE GINGER-TURMERIC YOGHURT

3 cm piece fresh ginger, grated

½ tsp ground turmeric or 1 tsp grated
   fresh turmeric

¾ cup full-cream yoghurt

Pinch of salt

FOR THE SMOOR

2 Tbsp vegetable oil

1 large onion, chopped

1 medium carrot, peeled and grated

1 cinnamon stick

1 star anise

2 cloves

2 cans chopped tomatoes (or equivalent
   in fresh tomatoes, grated or chopped)

½–¾ cup vegetable stock

2½ Tbsp uncooked Israeli couscous

1 can chickpeas, drained

1 Tbsp preserved lemon (optional)

⅓ cup dates, currants, raisins or sultanas

Salt and white pepper, to taste

TO SERVE

A large handful (80–100 g) of rocket leaves

1 Tbsp extra-virgin olive oil

Pinch of salt

Make the Ginger-Turmeric Yoghurt by stirring together the ginger, turmeric, yoghurt and salt in a small bowl. Set aside.

To make the Smoor, heat the oil in a medium-sized saucepan over medium heat and add the onion. Cook for 5–7 minutes, stirring from time to time, until the onion is translucent. Add the carrot, cinnamon stick, star anise and cloves, and cook, stirring for another 2 minutes. Stir in the tomatoes, stock and couscous, and allow the mixture to bubble away gently for another 10–12 minutes, stirring to be sure the couscous does not stick to the bottom of the pot. You might want to add another ¼–½ cup of stock if the mixture looks too thick. Add the chickpeas, preserved lemon (if using) and dates, and cook for another 3 minutes. Test for seasoning, adding salt and pepper as needed.

Spoon the Smoor into soup plates or a serving bowl and top with generous spoonfuls of the Ginger-Turmeric Yoghurt. Pile the rocket leaves on top, drizzle with olive oil and a pinch of salt, and serve immediately.

SERVES 4–6

Carrot Fries

These fries are moreish. You could dust them with Dukkah Spice Blend (p. 16), your favourite spice blend or simply season them with salt and pepper. Cut 'skinny' fries for elegant contemporariness! I sometimes pile these on top of dressed cos lettuce, sprinkle on dukkah dust or a herb salt and call it supper.

500 g carrots
¼ cup cornflour or rice flour
¼–½ cup vegetable oil
1 tsp sea salt
2 tsp chopped fresh dill
Zest of ½ lemon or orange, grated (optional)
Freshly ground black pepper
A tiny sprinkle of vinegar, to finish (if that is what you like on your fries)

Preheat the oven to 200°C and line a baking sheet with baking paper.

Cut the carrots into fries about 1 cm thick. Using a large mixing bowl, toss the fries with the flour. Toss again with the vegetable oil to coat the carrots.

Spread the coated carrots in a single layer on the baking paper. Bake the fries for 35–45 minutes, checking them from time to time and turning the tray and the fries as needed, to ensure they are well-coloured.

Mix the salt, dill and lemon or orange zest (if using) to create a herb salt. Tip the cooked carrot fries into the large mixing bowl (again) and toss with the herb salt. Grind over a little black pepper and finish with a sprinkling of vinegar, if you like.

SERVES 4 (AT A PUSH)

Linguini with Pork Sausage Balls, Courgettes, Spring Onion & Whipped Feta

Yes. It is as good as it sounds. And not at all schleppy *to make.*

Salt

500 g linguini pasta

450 g pork sausages or 'sizzlers'

1 scant Tbsp vegetable oil

200 g courgettes, very well washed and dried (with a clean kitchen towel) and chopped into 1½ cm pieces

4 spring onions, white + ½ green parts, finely sliced

30 g fresh mint leaves, shredded (not too roughly, though; you do want to be gentle with mint. It is extremely sensitive by nature)

Juice and zest of 1 lemon

Flaked salt and white pepper

¾ cup Whipped Feta (p. 46)

TO SERVE

Extra-virgin olive oil, to garnish

Freshly ground black pepper

Bring a large pot of water to a boil over high heat. Add a good handful of salt and the linguini pasta to the water and cook the pasta until al dente. Drain and set aside.

Snip the skin off the end of each sausage and pinch out little balls of the meat 2–3 cm in size. In a pot or a deep pan, add the vegetable oil and fry these rough little sausage balls over high heat, stirring from time to time so that they get good colour all round. After about 5 minutes, when the balls are mostly cooked through, add the courgettes and let them cook along with the sausage balls. Do not be tempted to add more oil; there is enough right there with the sausages. After the courgettes have been frying for 4 minutes, they should have some colour and be cooked through.

In a large mixing bowl, using 2 wooden spoons, add the cooked linguini, along with the sausage balls and courgettes. Add the spring onions, mint, lemon juice and zest, flaked salt and white pepper, and gently toss with the spoons to move the vegetables through the pasta.

Spoon the Whipped Feta over the hot pasta but do not toss through (unless you really want to). Pour a little olive oil over the Whipped Feta and, on the roughest setting, grind over a healthy amount of black pepper (feta and pepper are particularly good friends). The creamy feta will spread through the pasta as people serve themselves.

SERVES 4–5

Tamarind Salmon
with Orange, Chilli & Coriander

Full of hope for a return to entertaining, parties, clinking glasses of bubbly, laughter and sharing, I offer this sticky salmon. For a smaller group, one could cut smaller pieces instead of the whole side. The recipe is so easy, striking and delicious, you'll most certainly want it in your arsenal for wooing visitors or for a festive treat.

FOR THE TAMARIND-FIG CHUTNEY

1½ tsp fine cumin

¾ cup tamarind sauce

¼ cup smooth fig jam

½ tsp chilli powder

2 tsp Kikkoman soya sauce

FOR THE SALMON

Juice of 1 orange

Zest of 2 oranges – 1 grated, the other
   finely sliced

3 Tbsp marmalade

100 g butter

1 large fresh red chilli, seeds removed and
   finely chopped

Salt and white pepper, to taste

1 whole salmon fillet, ± 1kg (a side of salmon)

Large bunch (± 40 g) fresh coriander

To make the Tamarind-Fig Chutney, toast the cumin in a small pan until it becomes fragrant and a shade darker. Stir in the tamarind sauce and fig jam until the mixture is smooth and heated through. Remove from the heat and add the chilli powder and soya sauce. Pour the hot sauce into a sterilised jar and seal immediately.

Preheat the oven to 200°C.

In a small pot, stir together ¼ cup of the Tamarind-Fig Chutney, orange juice, grated orange zest, marmalade and butter. Place over low heat to simmer for about 5 minutes until saucy. Remove from the heat, add the chopped chilli and season with salt and white pepper.

Lay the salmon on a baking sheet lined with baking paper. Using a spoon, spread ¼ cup of the sauce all over the salmon, making sure it is entirely covered. Bake in the oven for 10 minutes. If you wish to slice the side into smaller pieces (125 g each), bake for no longer than 8 minutes.

Using two long spatulas, transfer the salmon to a serving platter. Scatter with the finely sliced orange zest and sprinkle generously with lots of fresh coriander. If you have extra sauce, serve it in a jug alongside. Green Beans with Crispy Garlic, Butter and My Insane Crumbs (p. 24) and Smashed Roasted Potatoes (p. 53) would go splendidly with this dish.

SERVES 5–7

[6]

I make lunch for my Sweetheart now

Like so many other workers, my husband, for a while the sole breadwinner, assumed more permanent occupation of his man cave-turned-home office. Remote support that he had installed for his clients long before lockdown became the real milieu in which he now worked. Instead of the school-lunch sandwich I sent him off with most mornings, or the nasty pie from the garage across from his office, I got to make him lunch! Amid bewilderment, uncertainty and the ordeal of closing my business, we clung to each other; ever my rock, my sounding board, my wise counsel and my mate, his love and belief the steady safety in my vulnerability.

Love is about sharing and appreciating little moments. It is about service, steadfastness and cherishing. We had a new appreciation for this little time together over lunch. Sometimes, we even got to sit down together and share one of his home brews. I got to make something nice for him! In the middle of the day!

Cold Sesame Noodles

This dish is Spartan in appearance but terrifically accurate in its conquest. This kind of simplicity is the way I want to eat.

1 Tbsp sunflower oil

100 g Chinese egg noodles, or other
   thin noodles

4 Tbsp Deeply Roasted Sesame Sauce (p. 13)

Chilli oil, to garnish

4 Tbsp Walnut Chilli Crisp (p. 129) or 2 Tbsp Lao
   Gan Ma Chilli Crisp

4 tsp toasted sesame seeds, to garnish

2 spring onions, very finely sliced on the diagonal,
   or very finely julienned (all the green too),
   to garnish

OPTIONAL ADDITIONS

Blanched or stir-fried broccoli or kale

Heat the oil in a small saucepan until just simmering then remove from the heat. Pour into a large bowl and leave to cool.

Cook the noodles according to the package instructions, with no salt or oil in the water. Drain the noodles (do not rinse them!) then tip them into the large bowl with the cooled oil and toss to coat. Lay the noodles out on a baking tray, uncovered, to cool. Refrigerate until cold. If you are storing the noodles in the refrigerator for longer than an hour, you will need to cover them.

Divide the noodles between two deep bowls. To serve, hold a fork or some chopsticks upright in the middle of the bowl of noodles. Twist the bowl to form a 'cone' of noodles. Pour a generous amount of Deeply Roasted Sesame Sauce down one side of the noodle cone. Drizzle the chilli oil over the noodles, allowing a little to puddle over the sesame sauce. Spoon over the Walnut Chilli Crisp for each bowl of noodles and sprinkle generously with the toasted sesame seeds. Finish with spring onions and broccoli or kale, if using, over the top of the noodles, and enjoy. You will need chopsticks, of course!

SERVES 2

Lamb Croutons

Eating a slice of roast lamb or a melting piece from a shoulder is one thing, but what everyone really wants are the caramelly, crispy, fatty bits at the edges. Lamb finds another whole permutation when it is torn and fried in a hot pan. At The Kitchen, our colloquial word for this fry was 'screouw' – the lamb is truly sizzled using its own natural fattiness, recreating, as it were, those choice bits and the particular deep flavour found in those roasted peripheries.

5 cloves garlic – 2 whole and 3 finely minced
    or grated
¼ cup extra-virgin olive oil
¼ cup + 1 Tbsp vegetable oil
4 slices stale bread (ciabatta, sourdough
    or country loaf), cut or torn into 1 cm pieces
1 onion, chopped
1 Tbsp Çemen Paste (p. 14), or 2 tsp Dukkah
    Spice Blend (p. 16), or your favourite spice rub
1 tsp za'atar or ¼ tsp dried thyme
2–3 cups cooked lamb, shredded
2 Tbsp freshly squeezed lemon juice
Maldon salt and black pepper, to taste
Drizzle of Tahini Dressing (p. 12), or similar
3–4 cups greens of your choice, or a mix of
    shredded spinach, baby spinach, coriander,
    chives and Italian parsley

Keep a serving platter warm in a low oven (100°C).

Make a little garlic oil by frying 2 whole cloves of garlic in a mix of the olive oil and ¼ cup of vegetable oil over medium heat until the garlic colours. Add the cubes of bread, stirring well to coat them in the garlic oil. Fry the bread for 2–3 minutes, until you have croutons. Remove from the pan and drain on paper towel.

Heat 1 tablespoon of vegetable oil in a broad pan over high heat and fry the onion. As it begins to colour, add the minced garlic and the Çemen Paste (or spice rub) and fry for another minute. Add the za'tar or thyme, then add the lamb and fry, stirring occasionally for 3 minutes. You want to get some good frazzled bits! Stir in the lemon juice and simmer for another minute or so, then season generously with Maldon salt and black pepper.

Tip the lamb onto the warm serving platter. Tumble the croutons over the lamb and drizzle the whole dish with a little of your preferred dressing. Finally, pile the greens on top of the croutons and serve.

SERVES 4

Melting Eggplant Pasta

Why resist the yielding disintegration of eggplant? This is a recipe I often long for and the reason I always pick up eggplant from the market. I have made many recipes with eggplant but this one, adapted from Francis Lam's recipe in Food52's Genius Recipes, releases eggplant to meltiness. It is my bowl of comfort.

⅓ cup extra-virgin olive oil, plus more
   to drizzle
4 cloves garlic, slightly squashed with the
   flat of a knife
500 g eggplant, cut into 1½ cm cubes
½ tsp dried oregano, thyme or za'atar
1 cup chicken or vegetable stock
1 packet (500 g) of spaghetti
Salt and freshly ground black pepper, to taste
2 tomatoes, diced
10 fresh basil leaves, very finely snipped

Pour the olive oil into a large, heavy-bottomed saucepan and add the garlic cloves. Set the pan over low heat and cook until the garlic colours a little. You absolutely do not want the garlic to burn. By the time you are done, it will have all but disintegrated and become (an ecstatic) one with the eggplant.

When the garlic becomes fragrant, add the eggplant and stir through the oil. Turn up the heat to medium-high, add the oregano (or thyme or za'atar) and cook for about 8 minutes, until softened. Add the stock and let it come to a boil, then lower the heat to medium-low. Partially cover the pot while the eggplant simmers (and disintegrates), for another 15–20 minutes. Stir from time to time to be sure the eggplant does not stick to the bottom of the pot.

In the meantime, boil the spaghetti in plenty of salted water until al dente and drain in a colander.

Season the now mostly melted eggplant with salt and black pepper. You may want to mash it up some more with a spoon. The eggplant will have yielded into oily, garlicky, silky lusciousness.

Toss the eggplant through the spaghetti, stir through the fresh tomato and most of the basil leaves. Top with the remaining basil leaves and drizzle with olive oil.

SERVES 4–5

Roast Leeks
with Anchovy & Soft-Boiled Eggs

This is an elegant dish, complete in its neat simplicity. Eggs and anchovy are, of course, a champion marriage.

1 bunch of leeks (3 large or 5 medium), trimmed
    and washed but kept whole

Extra-virgin olive oil, for roasting, + 3–4 Tbsp

Salt and black pepper, to taste

6 anchovy fillets

2 Tbsp lemon juice

2–4 medium-soft (boiled for 7 minutes) eggs

Flaked sea salt, to taste

Chives or dill, or any other herb you
    might have on hand

My Insane Crumbs (p. 173), to garnish

Preheat the oven to 200°C.

In a large pot of boiling water, blanch the leeks for 3 minutes. Remove from the pot and allow to cool. Then, slice the leeks in half lengthways and wash gently under cold water to remove any remaining traces of grit.

Line a baking sheet with baking paper. Pour out a solid glug of olive oil onto the baking paper. Season the oil with salt and pepper and use the cut side of the leeks to spread the oil around the baking sheet. The plan is to get the leeks well coated in the seasoned olive oil. Position the leeks close together on the baking sheet and roast for 12–15 minutes. They should be quite soft and melty with brown caramelised bits around the edges.

Mash the anchovies with the lemon juice in a small bowl. Stir in 3–4 tablespoons of olive oil. Using your hands, toss this anchovy mixture with the roasted leeks until well coated.

Arrange the leeks on a platter (or 2 plates), drizzling over every last drop of lemony anchovy. Roughly break the boiled eggs into chunks and arrange them on top of the leeks. Season with flaked sea salt and black pepper, and chives or dill, if you have any on hand. Finish with a generous sprinkling of My Insane Crumbs.

SERVES 2–3

NOTE:

A cheat/very good idea would be to use the Tonnato Sauce (p. 13) in place of the anchovy-lemon mix. It would do no harm to finish with a little shave of parmesan on top. The Caper Sultana Relish (p. 10) would also work tremendously well here.

Skirt Steak with Caper Sultana Relish

I have always had leanings towards ingredients, cuts and objects that are overlooked, hence my large collection of objects (including, to my family's distress, sofas and plates) looking for another lease on life. My favourite cut of steak, hardly an old thing, does not get as much attention as its brothers Rump, Sirloin, Rib Eye and Fillet. But flashed over hot coals for mere minutes, you will not find a more satisfying morsel! Its shape and the clarity of its grain might give you an inkling of its tenderness. I rub the skirt steak with salt and white pepper, and it lends itself to a great sear.

450 g skirt steak
Salt and white pepper, to taste
2 Tbsp sunflower oil
¼ cup Caper Sultana Relish (p. 10)
Extra-virgin olive oil, to drizzle

First, be sure your steak is dry. Use paper towel to pat it dry if it isn't. This makes for a better sear.

Next, you will need hot coals or a hot cast-iron pan.

If cooking in a pan, rub the steak with salt and white pepper. Then, allow your pan to become very hot. Add the sunflower oil and lower the steak into the pan with tongs. Squash the steak down onto the surface of the pan with a handy spatula or tongs to get a good sear. Open windows and doors – it will get smoky!

If cooking over hot coals, rub the steak with oil, salt and white pepper. Cook the steak for 2–4 minutes on each side – NO LONGER!

Once cooked, place the steak on a board and allow to rest for 5 minutes before slicing. Slice the steak against the grain and spoon over the Caper Sultana Relish, along with a drizzle of olive oil, if you care to.

SERVES 4

Dhal with Brussels Sprout Chhonk

This dhal is a comfort staple in our home. It is refreshingly unchallenging. What is exciting is the tempering, the chhonk that gets poured on top – typically ghee with mustard seed and curry leaf or ghee with cumin and chilli, and any number of other permutations. This layering is what I love most about creating a dish, where flavours swim beside and around each other, like moving through warm and cold currents in a mountain pool. Together these layers make a glorious whole!

FOR THE DHAL

3 Tbsp vegetable oil

2 onions, sliced

4 cloves garlic, sliced

4 cm piece fresh ginger, minced

1 cinnamon stick

3 cardamom pods

½ tsp fennel seeds, or 1 Tbsp coriander seeds,
   or both

2 tsp ground turmeric

1 carrot, grated

200 g Masoor dhal (red lentils)

1 fresh red chilli, halved lengthways

2 tsp vegetable stock powder

1½ tsp salt

3 cups water

FOR THE BRUSSELS SPROUT CHHONK

3 Tbsp vegetable oil

150 g Brussels sprouts,
   cut in half and washed

Salt, to taste

50 g ghee

2 tsp mustard seeds

¼ cup fresh curry leaves

10 g finely sliced garlic

OPTIONAL TOPPINGS

¼ cup either chutney, tomato sauce,
   yoghurt or coconut milk

Your favourite relishes, pickles and
   fresh herbs

To make the Dhal, heat the vegetable oil in a medium-sized pot that is deep enough in which to do some stirring. When it is hot, add the onions, garlic, ginger, cinnamon, cardamom, fennel and/or coriander seeds, and turmeric, and fry for 12–15 minutes, until the onion is translucent and beginning to colour. Stir in the carrot, dhal, red chilli, stock powder and salt, and cook for another 3 minutes. Add the water, lower the heat and simmer for 20–30 minutes, stirring from time to time to prevent sticking. Put the lid on but leave it open a crack to release steam.

After 30 minutes, the dhal will have become very soft. Stirring will make it smoother, too. You can add more water if you want a soupier dhal. I like it a bit thicker so that it can hold the tempering that finishes it off. Transfer to a bowl, ready for serving.

To make the Brussels Sprout Chhonk, heat the oil in a wide, heavy-bottomed pan. When it is quite hot, add the Brussels sprouts and cook undisturbed for 3–4 minutes, until they begin to gain colour and a bit of sear in spots. Stir the sprouts for another 3–6 minutes to colour the other sides. When the Brussels sprouts are cooked and well coloured, tip them out of the pan and set aside. Season with salt.

To the same pan, add the ghee. When it is melted and quite hot, add the mustard seeds and curry leaves and stir, cooking for a minute. The curry leaves will lose their greenness but do not be alarmed. Add the garlic, cook for a few seconds so that it just becomes acquainted with the ghee, then immediately add the cooked Brussels sprouts. Cook for another 30 seconds, stirring constantly. Pour the entire contents of the pan over the dhal in its serving bowl.

SERVES 4–6 (WITH LEFTOVERS)

2-ingredient Naan

320 g self-raising flour
280 g full-cream yoghurt
½ tsp salt
Sunflower oil, for shallow frying

In a large mixing bowl, stir all the ingredients together until you have a smooth, wet, sticky dough.

Tip the dough out onto a well-floured board or counter and knead briefly to bring the dough together.

Flour your hands and roll the dough into a long sausage. Then, using a dough cutter or knife, cut the dough into 12–15 equal pieces, depending on what size you'd like the naan to be. Roll out each piece into an oblong shape no more than 5 mm thick.

Fry each naan in sunflower oil in a pan.

MAKES 12–15

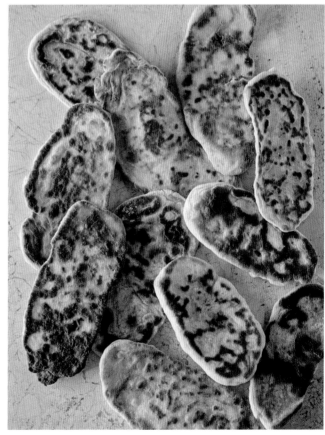

Tomatoes that have let themselves go...

Months of not really leaving the house, bra-lessness and an affinity for sweatpants... I cannot really say this was my experience. I am a person who likes to get dressed every day and put on lipstick. And in truth, I had too much going on. You could say that some people 'let themselves go' but found a new freedom as they dealt with re-shuffling priorities and a new approach to work, life and relationships. When you dress tomatoes, they tend to immediately let themselves go. But this need not be bad. Perhaps they simply become more of who they truly are.

Rescued Tomatoes

4 rosa tomatoes (jam tomatoes),
   or any tomatoes that need rescue
2 cloves garlic, minced
1 tsp salt

Cut the tomatoes in half lengthways and scoop out the seeds. Cut the tomatoes into thin strips, place in a medium-sized mixing bowl and combine with the garlic and salt.

The tomatoes will undergo something of a religious experience with the garlic and salt. You will find them much more pliant and amenable towards other foods, no matter what sort of sad (over or under ripe) condition they were in at the start.

SERVES 4

Japanese Tomato Salada

1 cup finely chopped red onion
1 tsp grated ginger
2 Tbsp sesame oil
2 Tbsp soya sauce
2 Tbsp rice vinegar
2 tsp sugar
1 tsp salt
A good grinding of black pepper
1 kg ripe tomatoes
20 g chives, snipped, for garnish (optional)

To make the dressing, whisk together the onion, ginger, sesame oil, soya sauce, rice vinegar, sugar, salt and pepper in a bowl until well combined.

Slice the tomatoes and arrange the slices on a salad platter or on individual salad plates. Spoon the dressing over the tomatoes and sprinkle with the snipped chives, if using.

SERVES 4–6

Garlicky Fennel Tomatoes with Anchovy

½–¾ cup extra-virgin olive oil

2 Tbsp fennel seeds, crushed

1 tsp dried chilli flakes

2 cloves garlic, squashed

8 anchovy fillets

¼ cup squashed pitted olives

Peel of 1 orange (optional)

1 kg smallish, very ripe red tomatoes, sliced

¼ cup red wine vinegar

Flaked sea salt and freshly ground black pepper, to taste

Heat the olive oil in a small pot over medium heat. Add the fennel seeds, chilli flakes, garlic and anchovies. Stir and swirl the ingredients together for 2–4 minutes, until the fennel is fragrant and toasty, the anchovies melted and the garlic cloves have some colour. Remove from the heat and set aside. Add the olives and orange peel, if using.

Lay out the sliced tomatoes on a beautiful platter or shallow salad bowl. Drizzle with the red wine vinegar. Spoon over the toasted fennel oil and season with flaked salt and black pepper to taste.

SERVES 6

[7]

Curiosity and hunger

In trying to imagine what I would do after being a restaurateur and a caterer, I came to a decision, not out of any bravery but out of trauma, to be honest. I decided that I would not open another restaurant or do catering ever again. What was a little brave was that I made a conscious decision to do things that would bring me, and hopefully others, joy. How would I earn a living? There were offers and ideas, open spaces and opportunities, and always, in my body, the constant yearning to make food for people.

I am a chef with a compelling curiosity – about food, about people and especially about where the two intersect. My hunger for knowledge and my curiosity keeps me in a constant state of openness and learning. I experiment, I pimp and hack recipes, and I seek out ways to live well and make things more delicious. Not having a restaurant opened my time and terrain! To explore and find fresh solutions too!

Staying curious and hungry means that there are so many people to learn from and so much to try. It keeps me in a happy, Socratic state. I honour my experience and my instincts but revel in the unfolding, learning and striving to know more and do better.

The Giant Sausage Roll

Give the people what they want, I say! And what do the people want? Banana bread and sourdough, pizza, lots of cheese and, after a global wave of loss, sadness, confusion and grief, a little comfort. Consolation. This shattering of puff pastry crumbs and the fatty sausage meat offers just that – with a side of English mustard and tomato sauce. I will take this little consolation any day, thank you! Share with friends when you are ready for entertaining, with a great big leafy salad alongside! I have adapted this recipe from one by Jill Dupleix.

200 g baby spinach

1 Tbsp vegetable oil

500 g pork sausage meat (you will need to squeeze this out of the sausage casings)

1½ slices stale white bread soaked in 2 Tbsp milk

2 cloves garlic, finely grated

1½ tsp smoked paprika

1 tsp celery seeds (ajwain) (optional)

Pinch of dried chilli flakes

3 Tbsp chopped fresh parsley

3 Tbsp chopped fresh dill

1 tsp salt

½ tsp black pepper

1 egg, beaten

Flour, for dusting

1 roll (400 g) frozen puff pastry, thawed

Preheat the oven to 200°C.

In a hot wok or pan, stir-fry the baby spinach in the vegetable oil. Allow the spinach to cool, then squeeze out some of the moisture and chop.

To a large mixing bowl, add the sausage meat, milk-soaked bread, garlic, paprika, celery seeds (if using), chilli flakes, parsley, dill, salt, black pepper and half of the beaten egg. Mix well using your hands. Mix in the spinach, aiming for islands of green rather than an even distribution of spinach.

Dust a work surface with flour and lay out the roll of puff pastry. Spread the mince mixture over the pastry dough. Roll the dough across the full length of the sheet into a log. Bring the pastry up around the meat and seal the edge with some egg.

Place the sausage roll seam-side down on a baking sheet lined with baking paper. Make a few small scores in the top of the pastry. Brush the roll with the remaining egg. Bake for 40 minutes, or until cooked through and golden.

SERVES 6

NOTE:

You can swap the pork sausage meat for beef mince with a 70:30 ratio of mince to fat. Some add cheese or fennel and coriander seeds, and herbs like sage and oregano, to the mixture. You can play!

Kimchi Fritters

Yes, I do make my own kimchi. I add a lot of ginger and julienned apple or pear, as well as chives and spring onions. I have a massive basin and I have bought big jars for storage. I use Table Mountain stones to weigh down the cabbage in the jar. My children do not approve of these jars of 'fermented business' perpetually occupying (squatting, they've said!) the dark corner of our kitchen. But I love the process. And I use my kimchi as pickle, toast topping and, here, for fritters! Kimchi 'juice', the liquid from the ferment, can transform a dressing! You can use home-made or store-bought kimchi for this recipe.

80 g self-raising flour

40 g rice flour

150 g kimchi

1 Tbsp chopped fresh coriander

Pinch of chilli powder or ½ tsp gochujang paste

¼ tsp salt

3 cups sunflower oil

Mayonnaise, to serve (optional)

Mix the flours, kimchi, coriander, chilli powder and salt together until combined. Depending on how much liquid is in your kimchi, you might need to add a bit of cold water to form a stiff batter.

Heat the sunflower oil in a wok until bubbles form around a chopstick or skewer. Drop spoonfuls of the batter into the hot oil and fry for 3 minutes, until cooked through. Remove from the pan and drain on paper towel. Eat *just so* or with mayonnaise or Green Chutney with Chaat Masala (p. 26)

SERVES 8–10 AS A SNACK

Carrot Daikon Pickle

I suggest that you pickle. There are many recipes about but this one, perfumed with star anise, adds a wonderful dimension to just about any dish. This is my signature pickle liquid. You can customise it by adding any raw vegetables of your choice!

4 carrots, peeled and finely julienned
1 medium daikon, peeled and finely julienned

FOR THE PICKLING LIQUID
1½ cups white vinegar
½ cup sugar
1 tsp fennel seeds
1 tsp coriander seeds
1 tsp black peppercorns
2 star anise
1 tsp salt
2 cloves garlic, finely sliced

Sterilise your jars by putting them through your dishwasher then leaving them in a 100°C oven for 10 minutes. Put all the vegetables to be pickled in a large jar or 3 smaller jars.

To make the pickling liquid, add all the ingredients to a saucepan and bring to a boil.

Remove from the heat and pour over the vegetables in the jar. Seal the jar immediately with a lid (if you want to preserve your pickles) or leave to steep for 2–3 hours for a very quick pickle. If hot-sealing your jar, leave to cool and store in the fridge.

MAKES A VERY LARGE JAR (± 750 G)

NOTE:
You can add fennel bulbs, radishes, cauliflower and spring onions to your pickle, too.

Panko-ed Eggplant with Japanese Curry, K's Pickles & Herb Salad

The famous Japanese katsu sando *has seduced the world. Traditionally, it is a crispy, crumbed pork cutlet sandwiched between two slices of soft milk bread or served with rice and, often, a Japanese curry like the one I offer here. This eggplant version allows non-meat eaters to get in on the excitement, too – there is something beguiling about the creamy inside and crispy crumbed outside.*

The 'leggy' treatment of the eggplant is very exciting (more surface area!) but you could cut your eggplant into 1½ cm thick 'steaks' and use the same crumbing technique for ease of execution.

FOR THE CURRY

170 g butter, divided

3 onions, julienned

1 Tbsp garam masala

3½ Tbsp curry powder

2 tsp MSG (optional)

1 small star anise

1 apple, peeled and grated

1 Tbsp tomato paste

1 Tbsp (sticky) dark soya sauce

2 Tbsp Worcestershire sauce

3 Tbsp honey

3½ cups chicken stock

Start by making the curry sauce. (This recipe will give you a lavish amount and you will be very happy for it.) Add 90 g of butter to a large saucepan over medium heat. Once the butter has melted, lower the heat, add the onions and cook for 30–45 minutes, until the onions become translucent, then golden, then caramelised. If they start to stick to the bottom of the pot, add a splash of water to deglaze. Stir in the garam masala, curry powder, MSG (if using) and star anise, and cook for a good 3 minutes, making sure the spices are toasted with the onions.

Add the grated apple and tomato paste to the onion-spice mix and cook for a further 3 minutes. Stir in the dark soya sauce, Worcestershire sauce, honey and chicken stock. Allow the mixture to simmer for 2–4 minutes, stirring regularly to avoid catching.

Using an immersion blender, blend the curry sauce until smooth, then add the remaining butter (80 g) while blending, one tablespoon at a time. Keep the sauce warm or put aside and reheat when ready to serve. If you feel your sauce is too thick, thin it down by adding water as you reheat it.

FOR THE EGGPLANT

3–4 medium eggplants
¾ cup all-purpose flour
2 eggs, beaten
1½ cups panko breadcrumbs
3½–4 cups sunflower oil

Now for the Panko-ed Eggplant. Peel each eggplant. Cut each one in half and then into four long 'legs' so that each resembles an octopus, but retaining the calyx to hold the legs together.

Place the flour in one bowl, the beaten eggs in another and the panko breadcrumbs in a third bowl. Dust each leg of the eggplant with flour, then dip the whole eggplant in the beaten egg. You may need to use your finger or a brush to make sure each leg gets egged. Finally, hold the eggplant over the panko bowl like a flower and, using your hands, make sure you get the breadcrumbs all over the inside and outside of the eggplant so that each part has a good coating of crumbs.

Heat the oil over medium-high heat in a wok until hot. Gently lower the crumbed eggplant into the oil and lower the heat so that the eggplant cooks gently all over. Fry for 8–10 minutes on each side, being careful to not lose any breadcrumbs as you turn the eggplants (I use a combination of tongs and a spatula – be careful to turn the eggplant away from you, to avoid splashing hot oil). Once golden and brown in places, remove the eggplant from the pan and drain on a paper towel-lined plate.

To plate, place a puddle of warm curry sauce on a wide soup bowl or plate. Place the eggplant 'octopus' atop the puddle of curry. Alternatively, pour the curry sauce over the crumbed eggplant. Serve with a good pickle, dressing and a little mound of rice beside the eggplant. Along with the pickle, cos lettuce goes well with this dish.

SERVES 6–8

Soya-Mirin Marinated Eggs

These are snack perfection. The legendary jammy egg – great to have on hand for a 'proper' snack – prepared upfront and ready to roll! Crack on! The marinade is also brilliant for poaching chicken breasts.

6 refrigerated eggs
1 cup soya sauce
1 cup water
5 slices fresh ginger
¼ cup mirin
2 Tbsp rice vinegar
1 Tbsp sugar
5 cm piece kombu (optional)
1 Tbsp Shiro (Japanese white soya sauce, optional)
Pinch of either dried chilli flakes, togarashi seasoning, gomashio or toasted sesame seeds

In a medium pot, bring a generous amount of water to a boil.

Prick the fat, round side of each egg. (I have an actual egg pricker, because I am a committed egg person, but I find a drawing pin works well in a pinch.) Have a timer ready for a 7-minute cook. Using a large spoon, gently plop each egg into the boiling water and allow them to simmer for exactly 7 minutes. Stir the water gently for a few seconds as the eggs begin cooking; this centres the yolk in the white. Have an ice bath ready for the boiled eggs.

In the meantime, add the remaining ingredients to a tall, fat jar and stir to combine.

Once the eggs have finished cooking, remove immediately from the pot and place in the ice bath to arrest the cooking process. Once cooled, peel the eggs and put them in the marinade. Cover the jar with a lid and store, covered, in the fridge for 2–3 days.

These are wonderful in ramen or just on their own with a sprinkling of either dried chilli flakes, togarashi, gomashio or toasted sesame seeds.

SERVES 4

Persian Carrot-Cardamom Jam with Grapefruit, Chilli & Orange Blossom

When I hold a jar of this jam up to the light, its jewel colour brings joy and pride. You will find a hundred ways to use this glorious business: with pork chops, whipped feta, a cheeseboard, or atop things sweet and savoury.

1¼ cups water

500 g sugar

± 15 green cardamom pods, crushed and seeds extracted

1 cinnamon stick

Segments of 1 grapefruit

2 thin-skinned lemons, very thinly sliced and pips removed

600 g carrots, coarsely grated

½ tsp dried chilli flakes

2 Tbsp orange blossom water

In a deep, heavy-bottomed saucepan, boil the water and sugar, stirring constantly until the sugar dissolves. Add the cardamom and cinnamon stick, and boil for another 5 minutes. Add the grapefruit, lemon and grated carrots, and boil over medium heat for 30 minutes. Stir from time to time until the mixture is thick and sticky.

Add the dried chilli flakes and orange blossom water, and boil for another 5 minutes.

Pour the jam into sterilised jars and seal immediately. This jam keeps well. Refrigerate after opening.

MAKES 3 × 200 G JARS

Fennel Jam

I adore the anise-like flavour of fennel. I love the way the fine slices of fennel become translucent in the syrup of this jam. Fennel jam wants to be alongside cheese, sausages and even in burgers and sandwiches!

1 kg whole fennel (3–4 large bulbs), sliced

Pinch of salt

400 g light brown sugar

80 ml white grape vinegar

Finely slice the fennel bulbs and the thicker stems. Roughly chop the fennel fronds and set these aside.

Put a heavy-based saucepan over medium heat. Add the fennel and a generous pinch of salt. Add the sugar and vinegar and bring to a boil. Simmer for 20–30 minutes, stirring occasionally, until some of the liquid has evaporated and the fennel is sticky and jam-like. In the last 3 minutes of cooking, add the chopped fennel fronds.

Spoon the jam into 3 warm sterilised jars, pouring over every last bit of syrup, and seal immediately. Hot-sealing creates a vacuum that will allow your jam to last 3 months or more. Refrigerate after opening.

MAKES 3 × 200 G JARS

Walnut Chilli 'Crisp'

8 onions, thinly sliced

4 heads of garlic, peeled, separated into cloves and sliced

4 cups vegetable oil

4 cinnamon sticks

2 star anise, broken into pods

½ cup walnuts

2 × 5 cm piece fresh ginger, peeled and very finely chopped

6 Tbsp dried chilli flakes

1½ fresh red chillies, finely sliced

½ cup soya sauce

¼ cup castor sugar

1 tsp salt

Bring the onions, garlic, vegetable oil, cinnamon sticks and star anise to a simmer in a medium-sized saucepan over medium heat. Cook for about 1 hour, reducing the heat as needed to maintain a gentle simmer, stirring occasionally, until the garlic and onions are browned.

In the meantime, toast the walnuts at 180°C for 8 minutes. Once toasted, chop the walnuts.

Mix the ginger, chilli flakes, fresh chilli, soya sauce, castor sugar and salt in a medium-sized bowl. Strain the onion mixture through a fine-mesh sieve set over the ginger-chilli mixture and stir with the hot oil to combine. Let the garlic and onion cool in the sieve before stirring them into the oil. Stir in the toasted walnuts.

To use, stir the mixture before spooning over a dish.

This recipe lasts for weeks in the fridge, especially if you hot-seal the jars.

MAKES 3 × 200 G JARS

Gilgeori Toast (Korean Street Toast)

This innocuous-looking sandwich has been a smash hit in my family. I confess to buying ready-cut slaw for the very purpose of turning out these sandwiches at the lazy drop of a hat!

1 (heaped) cup finely sliced white cabbage

½ cup julienned (or roughly grated) carrot

1½ spring onions, finely sliced

½ tsp salt

Pinch of cayenne pepper or togarashi

2 large eggs, beaten

2 tsp mirin (optional)

4 slices regular white sandwich bread

4 tsp vegetable oil, divided

40 g butter, divided, for buttering and frying

1 tsp powdered sugar

1 rounded tsp berry jam, tomato-chilli jam,
   or similar

A squeeze of barbecue sauce or oyster sauce

Kewpie mayonnaise or regular mayonnaise,
   in a squeezy bottle

Salt, to taste

Combine the cabbage, carrot and spring onions in a medium-sized mixing bowl. Sprinkle with salt and cayenne pepper (or togarashi) and massage the vegetables with your fingers to soften. Stir in the beaten eggs and mirin (if using) and mix well.

Pop two slices of bread in your toaster and toast till golden.

Heat a non-stick frying pan over medium-high heat, and add 2 teaspoons of oil and a good pat of butter (about 10 g) to the pan. Tip half the vegetable-egg mixture into the pan and spread it out into a neat square the same size as your toast. You are essentially making a vegetable omelette filling for your toast! (This sandwich is so much more than the sum of its parts, though!) Once the omelette square has cooked on one side, about 2 minutes or so, carefully turn it over to cook on the other side, for another 2 minutes.

Meanwhile, lay out two slices of toast. Butter one side and sprinkle with the powdered sugar. Spread the other piece of toast with your jam of choice.

With a large egg flipper, place the cooked omelette square on the buttered and sugared toast. Immediately squeeze on the barbecue sauce or oyster sauce and mayonnaise. Place the remaining piece of toast, jam-down onto the sandwich. Resist eating until you've made the second sandwich, to share with your sandwich partner. Toast the next 2 slices, add the remaining 2 teaspoons of oil to the pan and repeat for the second sandwich.

Slice in half and eat immediately!

MAKES 2 SANDWICHES

'Waldorf' Crunch Salad with Gem Lettuce

An alternative take on a Waldorf, this salad is a textural delight! Use the lettuce to scoop the mightily exciting crunch – I love a salad with a vegetable utensil!

FOR THE BASE
¾ cup labneh or full-fat smooth cream cheese
Zest of 1 lemon, grated
¼ tsp grated garlic
¼ tsp salt

FOR THE CRUNCH
1 pear or 1 Pink Lady apple, cored, halved, and cut into small batons or triangles (toss with lemon juice if not using immediately)
1 celery stalk, peeled and sliced into long, thin half-moons
3 radishes, cut into small wedges
¼ cup sultanas
⅓ cup almonds, pistachios or hazelnuts, toasted (if using hazelnuts, rub them in a clean tea towel to remove the bitter skins)
A few celery leaves, torn (optional)

FOR THE SALAD
2 heads lettuce – a combination of baby gems and radicchio works well
100 g blue cheese, frozen

FOR A LITTLE DRESSING (IF YOU ARE NOT USING YOUR LEAVES AS UTENSILS!)
¼ cup yoghurt
½ tsp salt
Zest of 1 lemon
Freshly squeezed lemon juice
1 Tbsp red wine vinegar or sherry vinegar
Freshly ground black pepper, to taste

To make the base for the crunch, put the labneh in a small bowl and stir in the lemon zest, garlic and salt. Arrange this mixture in a mound on a serving platter.

Top the labneh with the crunch: the pear or apple batons, celery, radish wedges, sultanas, toasted nuts and celery leaves (if using). Plant the crunch elements in the labneh, pressing down on them gently so that they cake slightly around the labneh. Add a few celery leaves here and there over the crunch mound, if you like.

Arrange the lettuce and radicchio leaves over and around the crunch salad. Shave the blue cheese over the whole salad. Scoop up the crunch into the lettuce leaves.

If you choose to make a more classic Waldorf, using a knife and fork, make a little dressing by combining all the dressing ingredients. Toss the leaves with the dressing in a medium bowl, adding a splash of olive oil, if you like, before arranging them over the salad.

SERVES 4

[8]

The peace of toast

A thin piece of toast with cold butter is the only thing I ever long for. Toast is what I am all about. In all its crispiness, it meets a particular need. It is also a perfect method of sharing. I invite people, one at a time, to sit at my kitchen counter and have toast with me. This way, I offer gifts of friendship using the vehicle of toast. One friend shared Nigel Slater's quote: 'It is impossible not to love someone who makes toast for you.' There! You, see? Friendship, collaboration and an invitation to intimacy on the simplest device!

Recommended instruments for serving toast:

1. A toast rack
2. A generous cutting board
3. A butter knife (it is rounded)
4. Butter in a butter dish (let us get serious)

Bone Marrow Compound Butter

I fell in love with @sadd_papi. Well, his Instagram feed, really. There. I said it. He is one of the crop of young stars doing great things with food. I watch his nimble tattooed fingers working with neat precision. Watching him make bone marrow compound butter had me spellbound.

1½ Tbsp sunflower oil, divided
16 marrow bones (± 1.2 kg)
Salt and white pepper, to taste
± 250 g soft (not melted!) butter
½ tsp salt
Pinch of dried thyme (optional)

TO SERVE
1 clove garlic
1 slice toast
Maldon salt, to taste
Sprinkle of chiffonade parsley

Preheat the oven to 220°C.

Brush ½ a tablespoon of oil on a baking sheet lined with baking paper. Lay the marrow bones on the tray, drizzle with the remaining oil, and season with salt and white pepper. Roast for 15–20 minutes, until the marrow is bubbling and soft.

Have a kitchen scale ready. Place a container on the scale and tare the scale. When the bones are cool enough to handle, scoop out the marrow and place it in a container. Weigh the marrow that you have harvested, then place the marrow in the bowl of a food processor.

Weigh the same amount of butter as marrow and add the butter to the marrow in the food processor. Process the marrow and the butter together to form an exceptionally smooth compound butter. Add the salt and thyme (if using) and store in an airtight container.

To serve, scrape a garlic clove over your toast. Spread the compound butter on the toast. Sprinkle with Maldon salt and chiffonade parsley.

MAKES ± 350–400 G

Tomato Toast

Do not attempt tomato toast with a sad, half-green tomato. You need one that, at the very least, has been sitting out on your counter with its friends for a good number of days. Prize number one is a tomato from your garden or organic heirloom tomatoes from a market. Hold these up like the Holy Grail and say a little prayer of thanks for their sun-ripened blessedness.

When I heard of the first lockdown, my immediate instinct was: now we really must eat out of our garden! I thought, with tantalising wonder, of an agrarian economy and my chicken-rearing fantasy coming into full play. I instructed my Sweetheart to get busy with that hydroponic garden we had been speculating about. My husband-engineer-grower got busy! Our backyard transformed into lushness with the rewarding acoustics of rainwater pumped through the pipes. We have been harvesting and feasting ever since!

1 slice toast (or a flatbread)
Butter (obvs)
20 g cream cheese
Sliced tomato
Maldon salt and black pepper, to taste
Tahini Dressing (p. 12)
Crispy Roasted Chickpeas (p. 177)
   or Crispy Lentils (p. 172)
Best extra-virgin olive oil, to take it over
   the edge

Spread your toast or flatbread with butter. Spread the cream cheese to the very edges of the toast and arrange the sliced tomato over the cream cheese. Season with salt and black pepper. Drizzle over the Tahini Dressing and sprinkle with Crispy Roasted Chickpeas or Crispy Lentils. Drizzle with peppery olive oil to finish.

SERVES 1

**ALTERNATIVE BEDDINGS OR TOPPINGS
THAT WOULD LIKE TO BE WITH TOMATOES:**
Caper Sultana Relish (p. 10)
Anchovies
Caesar Wholegrain Mayonnaise (p. 12)

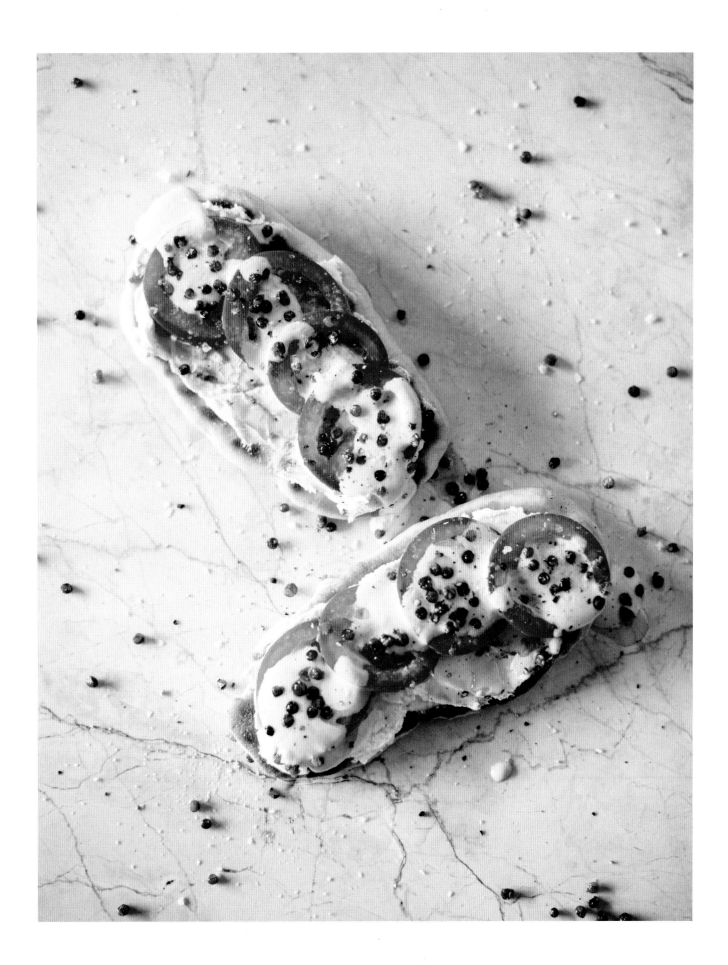

Kimchi Toast

I let my toast cool (use a toast rack or wave it about) before spreading over a generous amount of cold butter. Then I pile on the kimchi so that it is really Butter and Kimchi toast.

Garlicky Spinach

Tossing a bag (or harvest) of spinach and a little grated garlic in a hot wok is a standard source of greens in my home. On toast they become unctuous. Add a poached or 6-minute-boiled egg and you have breakfast, lunch or dinner!
Drizzle over any dressing or sprinkle away.

Cream Cheese or Whipped Feta (p. 46) with Carrot-Cardamom Jam (p. 128)

The creamy base is perfect for the sweet orange-blossomed sweetness.

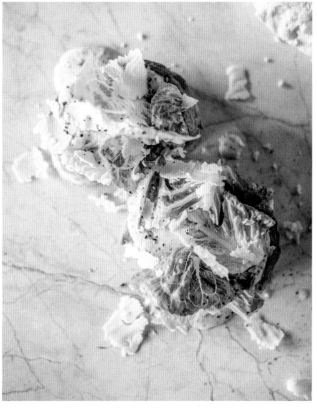

Caesar Wholegrain Mayonnaise (p. 12) with Eggs

In effect, this is a slightly deconstructed Caesar salad. You could make a lunch of it by topping with cos lettuce, an extra squeeze of lemon juice and shaved parmesan. Although I am a proponent of THIN crispy toast, in this instance, I would go for a thicker-sliced white country loaf or sourdough.

Gloopy Aubs

While you are making the gloopy eggplant for the Melting Eggplant Pasta (p. 100), it is a clever move to make extra eggplant while you are at it. The texture, on crispy toast with a small pile of herbs or bitter greens like wild rocket or mizuna, is sublime!

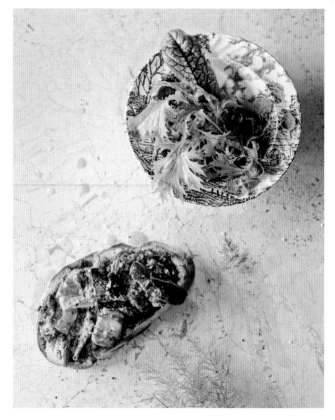

White Bean Tonnato

Buttered toast gets a generous spread of Tonnato Sauce (p. 13) and then olive-oiled cannellini beans. Sprinkle on some fresh parsley or herb of your choosing, drizzle on Caper Sultana Relish (p. 10) and boom! There you go!

Peanut Butter with Fatty Crispy Puffed Rice (p. 176) or Peanut Chutney Podi (p. 171)

Here, peanut butter gets a savoury crunch. A liberal topping of Peanut Chutney Podi with its lime leaf hook is quite addictive.

[9]

Earrings & lipstick for Instagram

After sadness, quiet and then resolve, I knew that I needed a little time away to ground my intention. At a friend's beautiful cottage in the country, I bathed in quiet, read and wrote.

Without a restaurant, I was unfettered and in my new found freedom there came this comfort: at The Kitchen I offered hospitality and exercised creativity. I could still do this! On a much larger platform, using tools like Instagram and YouTube. I could do what I had been doing all along, connecting with strangers and friends, and sharing my knowledge – only this time, globally! I could still be helpful, and I could have fun with it!

My kitchen became my studio, my Sweetheart became my cameraman and my son became my genius editor. Since I was making food in my kitchen anyway, we would simply film it in the moment, in the hope that it would be inspiring. All I needed were my earrings (no problem there) and lipstick (quick rush) and there, user @ capetownk was live online!

Vietnamese Tomato Salad

Will someone please fly me to Vietnam? I have asked before and I think it would be so nice. I have been good. I would like to walk through markets. I would like to pick herbs from the centre of a table and add them to a steaming bowl before me of something redolent with lemongrass and lime. Pho? Bánh mì? I would also like a proper Vietnamese coffee. Until then, I dream. This Nuoc Cham-dressed salad is a tenuous spectre of what could be, but delicious nonetheless!

500 g mixed heirloom tomatoes, halved if small or cut into wedges if large

1 small fennel bulb, thinly sliced

1 Persian cucumber, halved lengthwise and sliced into half-moons, or 3 small Lebanese cucumbers, cut on the diagonal

1 red onion, thinly sliced

½ cup Nuoc Cham Dressing (p. 10)

⅓ cup crushed salted dry-roasted peanuts (peanut roasting works best in an oven)

⅓ cup store-bought fried shallots or onions (or you can make your own – p. 176)

2 cups coarsely chopped mixed tender herbs (such as dill, coriander and/or basil)

Layer the salad ingredients, beginning with the tomatoes, then fennel, cucumber and red onion, drizzling the Nuoc Cham Dressing all over the salad as you go. Finish with the crushed peanuts, crispy onions and all those glorious herbs!

SERVES 4–6

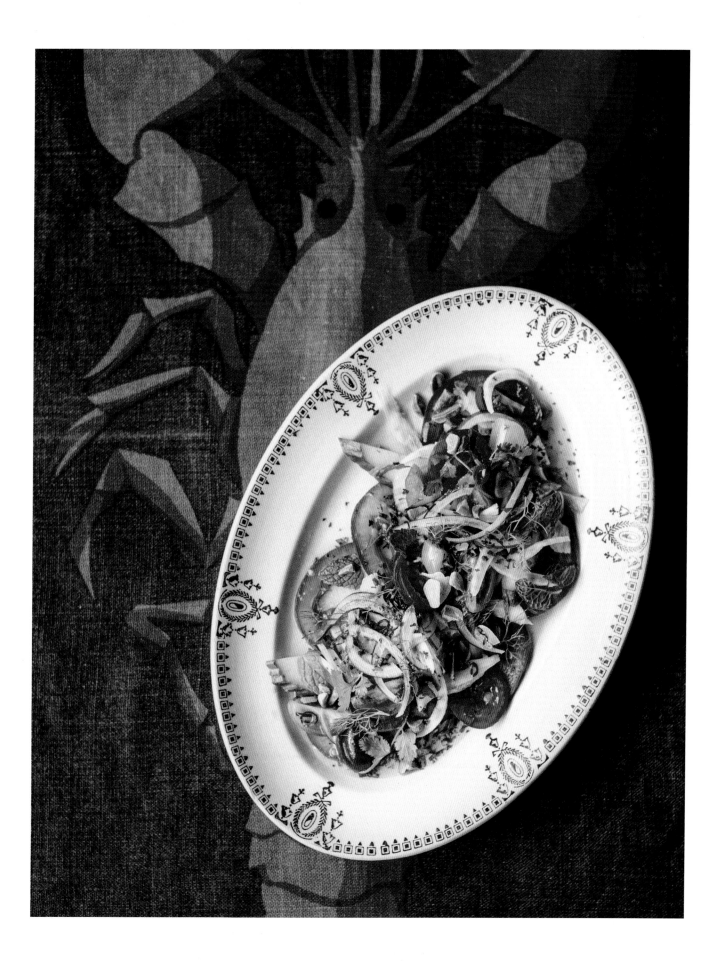

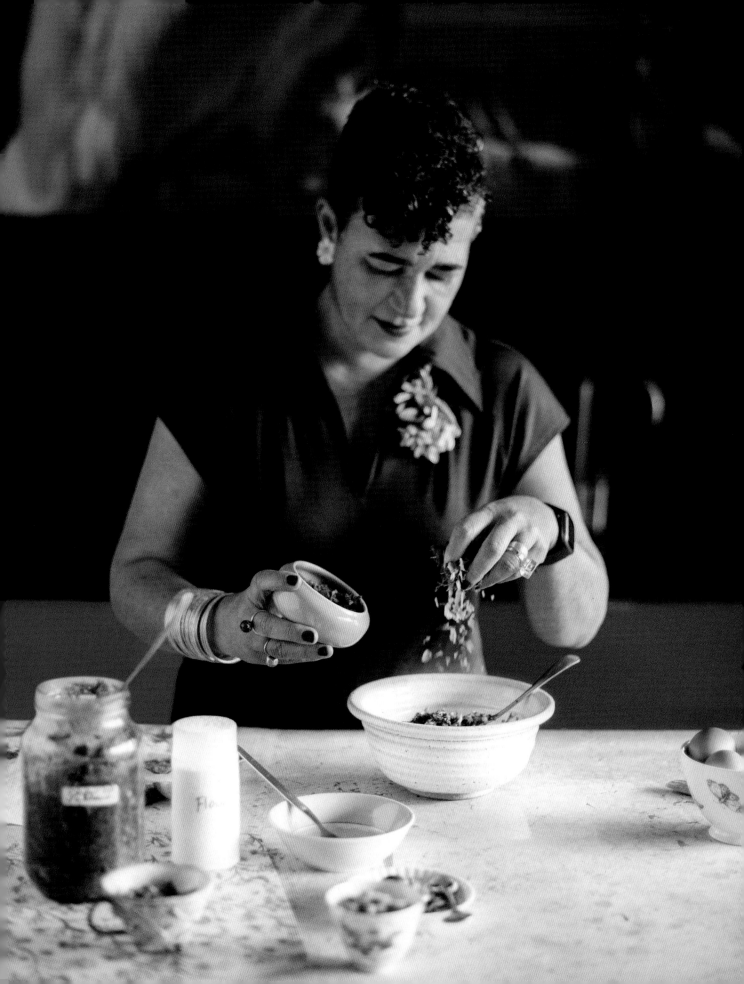

Tuna Egg Parcel

I am very enamoured of a parcel. Something about the secret inside creates a little frisson of excitement. In this case, a humble can of tuna along with other ingredients we love becomes the prize!

1 Tbsp sunflower oil, plus extra, for frying

2 onions, diced

1 can tuna, drained

½ cup pitted green olives, chopped

2 Tbsp Caper Sultana Relish (p. 10),
    or 1 Tbsp chopped fresh parsley + 1 Tbsp
    chopped capers

1 Tbsp fresh shredded mint

Salt and freshly ground black pepper, to taste

4 square spring roll wrappers

4 eggs for the parcels, plus 1 egg, beaten

Lemon wedges, to serve

Heat 1 tablespoon of oil in a pan. Once hot, fry the onions until translucent and fragrant. Remove from the heat and add the tuna, olives, Caper Sultana Relish and mint. Season with salt and black pepper.

Lay out a square of spring roll wrapper on a large, lightly floured board or work surface. Imagine dividing the square in two along the diagonal to form two triangle halves. With this in mind, spoon the tuna mixture onto one half, leaving a good amount of room to join the edges later. Create a little well in the tuna mixture and break an egg into the well.

Brush or use your finger to slightly dampen the edges of the pastry with some beaten egg. Fold the empty triangle half of spring roll wrapper over the tuna-egg mixture and pinch the edges of the wrapper together. You should be left with a large triangle with plenty of room along the edges. Brush these edges with beaten egg. Fold over the bottom two corners to create an open envelope, then fold the top corner over to close it. Seal with a little of the beaten egg.

Repeat this process for the remaining 3 wrappers.

Heat some oil in a frying pan. When it is sizzling, fry the parcels, two at a time, for about 2 minutes on each side. Remove from the pan and serve immediately with a good wedge of lemon.

MAKES 4 PARCELS

Warm Eggplant Salad with Red Onion, Crispy Garlic & Tahini

All done on one sheet, this salad makes a quick and pleasing meal. The little nubs of crispy garlic are a delight!

5 medium eggplants, cut into 2½–3 cm cubes
   (they will shrink)
2 red onions, cut into 3 cm chunks
6–8 cloves garlic, squashed with the flat side
   of a knife
½ cup sunflower or extra-virgin olive oil
3 Tbsp tahini
1 Tbsp freshly squeezed lemon juice
½–⅔ cup cold water
½ tsp dried chilli flakes
Flaked sea salt and black pepper, to taste
2 Tbsp toasted sesame seeds
2 Tbsp either moskonfyt, honey or pomegranate
   molasses (optional)
A handful of fresh mint or parsley leaves, to garnish
   (pick or chop these if you prefer)

Preheat the oven to 200°C.

Toss the eggplants, red onions and squashed garlic cloves with the oil in a large bowl and arrange in single file on a baking sheet lined with baking paper. Tuck the squashed garlic under some of the other vegetables for protection (they will become a little crispy while protected by their friends). Roast for 15–25 minutes, until all are tender and beautifully coloured.

Whisk the tahini, lemon juice, water, chilli flakes and a pinch of salt in a bowl until you have a lovely creamy dressing. Add more water if it is too thick. You can also use the Tahini Dressing (p. 12).

Arrange the roasted vegetables in a bowl or in a pile on a platter. Season with flaked sea salt and black pepper. Drizzle over the tahini dressing and scatter the toasted sesame seeds over the vegetables. If you would like a bit of sweetness, drizzle over the moskonfyt (or sweetener of choice). Garnish generously with the fresh mint or parsley. This pairs well with green beans on the side.

SERVES 4 (WITH GREENS BESIDE)

Corn & Persimmon Chaat Salad

Here is a salad that sings and dances like an Indian performer, full of colour, brightness and bells. I served it recently in tiny bowls as a 'mouth amuser' or amuse bouche. Persimmons and peaches are interchangeable in this recipe; use the freshest fruit in season!

3 mealies

2 medium-sized ripe persimmon, cut into
   1–2 cm pieces

½ red onion, cut into ½ cm chunks

2 fresh green chillies, thinly sliced

1 clove garlic, very thinly sliced

3 cm piece fresh ginger, peeled and julienned
   into matchsticks

⅓ cup roughly chopped fresh coriander

½ tsp freshly ground black pepper

2 tsp sugar, divided

2½ tsp chaat masala, divided

¼ cup fresh lime juice, or 2 Tbsp tamarind paste
   stirred with 2 Tbsp iced water

⅓ cup chopped salted and roasted peanuts

⅓ cup slangetjies (sev), or crushed potato chips

Stand the mealie upright in a medium-sized bowl and slice off the kernels with a sharp knife. Using the back of the knife, scrape along the cob to release the 'milk' into the bowl. Add the persimmon (making sure to get all the juices into the bowl too), red onion, chillies, garlic, ginger and coriander, and toss very gently to combine. Sprinkle with black pepper, 1 teaspoon of sugar and 1 teaspoon of chaat masala before tossing again.

Stir in the lime juice and remaining sugar and chaat masala in a small jug until the sugar dissolves. Add the water and stir to combine.

Spoon the salad into individual bowls or into a large salad bowl. Pour the iced lime and chaat water over the salad and top with the peanuts and slangetjies, then serve.

SERVES 4

Spanspek & Cucumber Salad with Nuoc Cham & Minty Coconut Gremolata

Spanspek (cantaloupe*) is my favourite fruit. I am always looking for ways to make it feel included in mainstream lunch fare. I think this salad is a great introduction! A traditional Italian favourite paired with Parma ham, here it is, fresh and moreish with Nuoc Cham Dressing. It is just glorious to present! When spanspek is not in season, papaya is a great substitute.

1 spanspek or papaya (± 1 kg), pips removed and sliced into 1½ cm half-moons

500 g skinny English cucumber, halved lengthways, each cut into 4 long strips and then into chunks

⅓ cup Nuoc Cham Dressing (p. 10)

¼ red onion, very finely sliced

1 fresh jalapeño, very finely sliced

½ cup Coconut Gremolata (p. 170)

½ cup of fresh, torn herbs, a combination of basil and mint

Juice of 2 limes and zest of 1

Flaked salt or fish sauce, to taste

Arrange the spanspek or papaya slices on a serving platter with the cucumber chunks tucked in here and there. Drizzle the Nuoc Cham Dressing generously over the salad, then scatter with the red onion and jalapeño. Sprinkle the Coconut Gremolata over the top of the salad along with the herbs. Sprinkle over the lime juice and all the lime zest you can muster. Finish with a scattering of flaked salt or an extra drizzle of fish sauce.

SERVES 4–5

*"Cantaloupe Island" is a jazz standard by Herbie Hancock (Blue Note Records). I love Us3's version, "Canteloop (Flip Fantasia)" (Blue Note Records).

Chana Flour & Butternut Pancakes

We are always looking for vegetables to use as a vehicle on which to pile salad and toppings. This is a really good one. You could add avocado or a fried egg, leftover shredded chicken or sausage – but always top with fresh, well-dressed leaves. Phew! A grounding pancake offers up a world of deliciousness! And instead of the toasted whole spices, you can use one of my Spice Blends (p. 16).

450 g butternut, peeled and coarsely grated

½ tsp fine sea salt

¼ tsp cumin seeds

¼ tsp coriander seeds

¼ tsp fennel seeds

4 large eggs

1 tsp ground cinnamon

1 tsp ground ginger

1 tsp sugar

1 clove garlic, minced

⅔ cup chana (chickpea) flour

½–¾ cup fresh coriander (leaves and
　stems) chopped

½ cup oil, for frying (about 2 Tbsp per pancake)

½ cup crème fraîche, full-cream yoghurt
　or labneh

3 Tbsp çemen paste + 1 Tbsp water (to make a
　dressing), or your favourite pesto or relish

½ red onion, very finely sliced

100 g wild rocket, watercress or mizuna

1 Tbsp olive oil, or Poppy Seed Vinaigrette (p. 12),
　or similar

Flaked sea salt and freshly ground black pepper,
　to taste

NOTE:
You could substitute the butternut with carrots.

Place the grated butternut in a colander and sprinkle with the fine sea salt. Mix the salt through the butternut, allowing it to draw out the moisture and soften a little. Leave this in the colander for 10–15 minutes, before squeezing out as much liquid from the butternut as you can. There won't be a huge amount but this step is important for making a crispy pancake.

Dry-fry the cumin, coriander and fennel seeds in a small pan until fragrant. Grind these toasted whole spices in a coffee grinder until fine.

Crack the eggs into a large mixing bowl and whisk. Add the freshly ground spices along with the cinnamon, ginger, sugar, garlic and chana flour. Whisk together, then stir in the butternut and coriander. Mix with a wooden spoon until thoroughly combined.

Heat a large frying pan over medium-high heat. Add 2 tablespoons of oil to the pan and fry ½–⅔ cup of the pancake mixture, spreading it about 1 cm thick as you go. Since I am addicted to crisp edges, I don't mind my pancakes being a bit 'frilly' on the edges but you can shape yours to perfect discs, if that is your proclivity.

Once you have fried all the pancakes, lay each one on a plate. Spoon on the crème fraîche and drizzle with the çemen dressing, or pesto or relish of your choosing. Scatter on some red onion and pile the wild rocket on top. Drizzle with olive oil or your favourite dressing (from this book!). Sprinkle on a little flaked salt and a light grinding of black pepper for the leaves.

SERVES 4

Fennel-Plum-Cucumber Salad with Shaved Gorgonzola

The little puckery tartness of the Sumac Dressing is a delicious burst of flavour with the plums in this salad. Oh, these little joys!

1 very skinny English cucumber, or a few Persian cucumbers (400–500 g), halved lengthways and sliced into thin half-moons

1 large fennel bulb (± 200 g), very finely sliced lengthways

1 stalk celery, peeled and sliced on the diagonal into long half-moons

2 ripe plums, pitted, halved and cut into thin wedges

3 Tbsp Sumac Dressing (p. 14) or similar

50 g baby lettuce leaves or tender herb mix

2 Tbsp crème fraîche (optional)

1 Tbsp extra-virgin olive oil

A few fennel fronds

A few celery leaves

50 g Gorgonzola cheese or Gorgonzola dolce, frozen

Flaked salt and freshly ground black pepper, to taste

2 Tbsp Crispy Mung Beans (p. 172) (optional)

In a large bowl toss the sliced cucumber, fennel, celery and plums with 2 tablespoons of the Sumac Dressing. Arrange these dressed vegetables artfully on a large platter.

Spread the lettuce leaves over the salad and dot spoonfuls of the crème fraîche over the salad, if using. When you are ready to serve, drizzle the whole salad with the remaining tablespoon of Sumac Dressing and olive oil. Arrange the fennel fronds and celery leaves over the salad and grate over the Gorgonzola using a microplane or fine box grater.

Season with flaked salt and black pepper, and sprinkle over the Crispy Mung Beans, if using.

SERVES 4

Caracara Orange, Date & Toasted Almond Salad with Rocket

I adore the pairing of orange, especially oranges of such marvellous colour, with other ingredients that I love: dates, almonds, rocket and parmesan. This salad is bold and beautiful and can hold its own as a starter or be part of a decent lunch beside a roast chicken.

20 almonds

4 caracara oranges

8 juicy pitted dates

2 Tbsp pure almond oil (or other nut oil
   or flaxseed oil)

16–20 shavings parmesan cheese

40 g rocket, to garnish

Flaked sea salt and coarsely ground
   black pepper, to taste

Lay the almonds on a baking sheet and place in the oven preheated to 180°C for 6–8 minutes, until fragrant and toasted. Chop roughly and set aside.

Using a sharp paring knife, peel the skins and remove the piths from the oranges, then slice all four.

Layer the salad, in the style of an elegant carpaccio, starting with the sliced oranges, then the dates and roughly chopped toasted almonds. Drizzle with 1 tablespoon of the almond oil, scatter over the parmesan shavings and, finally, add the pile of rocket in the middle. Drizzle the remaining nut oil over the salad and finish with flaked sea salt and coarsely ground black pepper.

SERVES 4

AN ALTERNATIVE SALAD

Replace the parmesan shavings, dates and rocket with finely sliced fennel, olives, red onion and mint. Sprinkle with Dukkah Spice Blend (p. 16).

[10]

The crispy topping and ASMR

I have a little theory: after an unprecedented, prolonged time in sweatpants and lying on the couch, people felt drawn to Crunch. ASMR (autonomous sensory meridian response) was having its moment (it is here now, people!) – an acoustic dimension to the eating experience that people never knew was possible, or that we simply had never articulated before! We have always known that smell and taste are intricately connected, but now sound, too!

I have been committed to finding the 'soul of the broccoli', and to looking to the frisson between flavours. I am even more interested in the nuance and layers of flavour within a dish. These can be heightened or diminished by texture, like overcooked lentils or undercooked eggplant. Who can resist the excitement of CRUNCH? I offer, in this chapter, recipes for play!

Coconut Gremolata

This is the topping that got me hooked on toppings. It is super fresh and therefore should be used straight away (on top of salads, rice or roasted vegetables) to add a little kick and texture. Please go ahead and create your own riff on this: a bit of chilli? A different herb? This one has a south-east Asian angle with the lime juice and fish sauce. You will get the idea quick-quick! And do not be alarmed by the addition of citric acid; it is a natural zing-bringer and preserver.

1 red onion, thinly sliced into rings

¼ cup all-purpose flour

⅓ cup sunflower oil

½ cup coconut flakes

1 Tbsp fish sauce

2 tsp freshly squeezed lime juice

¼ cup fresh chives, snipped (optional)

1 Tbsp finely grated lime zest

1 tsp citric acid

1 cup fresh mint leaves, snipped

Flaked sea salt and freshly ground black pepper, to taste

Preheat the oven to 180°C.

In a medium bowl, toss the red onion with the flour.

Heat the oil in a saucepan over medium-high heat. Add the flour-dusted onion rings and fry for 8–15 minutes, stirring occasionally, until brown and crisp. Transfer to a bowl or plate lined with paper towel.

Toast the coconut flakes on a baking sheet in the oven for 3–5 minutes. Transfer to a plate to cool.

Add the crispy onions to a medium-sized bowl. Season with the fish sauce and lime juice. Add the toasted coconut flakes, chives (if using), lime zest, citric acid and mint, and toss. Season with flaked sea salt and black pepper.

MAKES A TOPPING OF 5–6 SERVINGS

Peanut Chutney Podi

It is only love that compels me to share this recipe with you. This Peanut Chutney Podi (or pudi) is wildly addictive and frankly bewitching. When I need to use my full power of allure, I hand a little cannister of chutney podi over to my prey. Just one taste, eyes wide with surprise, and I know I have them under my spell! Do you understand now, the depth of my cunning and my method of seduction? Sprinkle it on toast for private pleasure.

1 cup peanuts

8 sprigs fresh curry leaves

6 cloves garlic, grated

1 small ball (just smaller than a table tennis ball) tamarind paste (the seedless, sticky paste, rather than tamarind in a jar)

1–2 Tbsp chilli powder

3 Tbsp jaggery (palm sugar)

Salt, to taste

1 tsp citric acid (optional)

My secret weapon: zest of 1 fresh makrut lime or 1½ tsp powdered Thai lime leaf

Toast the peanuts in the oven at 180°C for 7 minutes. Tip the toasted peanuts into a blender.

Place a pan or wok over medium heat and dry-toast the curry leaves, pulled from their sprigs. They will go crisp and dry. Add the garlic, tamarind paste, chilli powder, jaggery, salt, citric acid (if using) and makrut lime zest (or powdered Thai lime leaf) to the peanuts in the blender and pulse-blend until a rough powder forms. I prefer mine a little rougher so that I still get tiny bits of the peanuts but you can blend yours to a desired consistency. Store in an airtight container in the fridge.

MAKES 1½ CUPS

Crispy Lentils or Mung Beans

Talk about a healthy(ish) crunch! I discovered these as a result of sheer laziness: I left out some leftover cooked green lentils (about 1½ cups), laid out on a baking sheet, overnight, instead of packing them away in the fridge. No magic elves came to put them away and they were still there the next day. And there, on the stove, was a wok, also needing to be cleaned. (Hmm.) I poured some oil into said wok (a cup or 2) and spooned the now naturally dehydrated lentils into the hot oil. Some popping action ensued – thrilling! Lentils do not usually get this kind of excitement! I removed the lentils with my slotted spoon after 4 or 5 minutes. They were now decidedly crispy – hot and ready for seasoning opportunities. Welcome to my world, fried lentils!

I seasoned my lentils with salt and pepper, garlic powder and herbs. They make great friends with steamed and raw vegetables, bringing a snacky pop to any dish needing to be rescued from mundaneness.

1 cup green lentils
2 cups sunflower oil
Salt and pepper, or your seasoning
   of choice, to taste

Cook the lentils in plenty of boiling water for 13–15 minutes, until tender, then drain and rinse in a colander. Leave the lentils out to dry overnight or spread them out on a baking sheet lined with baking paper and dry low and slow in an 80°C oven for 30 minutes.

Heat the oil in a wok and fry the cooked and dried lentils, half a cup at a time, for 4–5 minutes, stirring the oil from time to time. Remove the lentils and drain on a plate lined with paper towel. Season with salt and pepper or any seasoning of your choice.

Mung beans get the same treatment, only they need to be cooked for 30–40 minutes, until tender, before being dehydrated and fried.

MAKES ± 1½ CUPS

My Insane Crumbs

Why are these insane? Well, I just like to go overboard sometimes! Having crispy breadcrumbs about, toasted with oil or butter, is no bad thing. From there, you pimp them with herbs or, in my case, parmesan cheese, lime leaf and crispy onions.

1 cup fresh breadcrumbs, made by blitzing day-old ciabatta in a food processor

¼ cup sunflower oil

2 Tbsp garlic flakes (or finely sliced cloves fried in a decent amount of oil until honey-coloured)

2 Tbsp grated parmesan cheese (optional)

Pinch of Chinese five-spice powder (or one of my 3 Spice Blends [p. 16])

Pinch of white pepper

¼ tsp salt

½ tsp powdered makrut lime leaf, or grated lime zest, or ½ tsp citric acid

2 Tbsp store-bought crispy onions, or use my Fried Onions (p. 176)

Fry the fresh breadcrumbs in the sunflower oil over medium-high heat, stirring constantly. The crumbs should start to turn golden-brown at around 4 minutes. Remove and allow to cool.

To a medium mixing bowl, add the garlic flakes, parmesan, Chinese five-spice, white pepper, salt, powdered lime leaf or lime zest and crispy onions. Mix together lightly with the fried breadcrumbs. Scatter this flavourful crumb over everything from fish, roast chicken, vegetables and salads.

MAKES 1¼ CUPS

Fatty Crispy Puffed Rice

This is a crisp that is perfectly at home atop eggs, rice, blanched or roasted vegetables, and on risottos and gratins. No snap, but crackle and pop, yes!

100 g bacon bits, frozen and lightly broken up, or streaky bacon, frozen and finely chopped

2 cloves garlic, grated

½ tsp fresh thyme or oregano

1–1½ cups unflavoured Rice Krispies or mumra puffed rice

Fine salt and freshly ground black pepper, to taste

Place the frozen bacon bits or streaky bacon in a food processor or blender and pulse once or twice until it resembles coarse breadcrumbs.

Fry the bacon, garlic and thyme (or oregano) for 2 minutes, until the bacon is cooked and has released some oil. Add the Rice Krispies (or puffed rice), stir to coat in the oil and fry, stirring continuously, for another minute, until the puffed rice has taken on some colour and is fragrant with the garlic, bacon oil and thyme. Remove and transfer immediately to a plate or baking tray to prevent burning. Season with salt and pepper to taste (it will be quite salty from the bacon but might need a pinch of additional salt).

MAKES 2 CUPS

Fried Onions the Way We Used to Do Them at The Kitchen

4 cups sunflower oil

2 cups all-purpose flour

½ cup rice flour

6 onions, finely sliced

Heat the oil in a wok over high heat.

Combine the flours in a medium-sized mixing bowl. Toss the sliced onions into the flour mixture, one handful at a time, breaking up the rings as you go so that each one is coated in the flour.

Fry the onions 1–2 handfuls at a time. Using a spider or slotted spoon, turn the rings over in the oil after a few minutes so that they become evenly golden.

Remove the onions with your spider spoon to a cooling rack set over a baking tray.

MAKES 2½ CUPS

Crispy Roasted Chickpeas

The trick to crispy chickpeas? Dehydration!

3–5 Tbsp extra-virgin olive oil

1 can chickpeas, thoroughly drained, rinsed and dried with paper towel or a clean dish towel

3 Tbsp either Dukkah, Thandai or Harissa Spice Blend (p. 16)

Preheat the oven to 200°C.

Line a baking sheet with baking paper and brush lightly with some olive oil. Spread the chickpeas in an even layer over the tray and roast in the oven, preferably on the fan setting, for 15 minutes to dehydrate the chickpeas (super dryness = super crispiness). Give the pan a shake at 8 minutes.

After 15 minutes, drizzle the remaining olive oil over the chickpeas on the baking sheet. Shake and stir the chickpeas to ensure they are evenly coated. Sprinkle your chosen Spice Blend over the chickpeas and stir them on the baking sheet to coat. Return to the oven and roast for an additional 5–12 minutes, until the chickpeas reach the crispiness you desire. Allow them to cool in the oven with the door cracked open; the gentle dry heat will ensure the chickpeas are crispy.

Store the roasted chickpeas in an airtight container or use immediately. They are great unadorned, perfect for garnishing hummus or for adding to other dishes like Pasta with a lot of Onions (p. 84)

SERVES 4

[11]

The truth of butter and sugar

I confess that when I want to eat a little something sweet, I want to eat it sooner rather than later. Baking demands a degree of discipline (hence my enduring regard for pastry chefs and bakers) and an obedience to the authority of the recipe, of science and of time.

The recipes that follow answer my need for something simple involving butter and sugar that can be made with some ease by a person who does not have a great deal of patience, and instead wants a perfect reward deferred within as little time as possible.

You will find a leaning towards lemony things, simplicity and 'things to have with tea'. There is an element of selfishness here: this selection is the butter and sugar that I enjoy.

New Lemon Squares

I will not deny that I came under a degree of small fire for not including The Kitchen's legendary Lemon Squares in any of my previous recipe books. Here is the thing: having shaped and tested the recipe many times before it even reached The Kitchen, our Lemon Squares took on a life of their own after hundreds of batches. An organic feat, with various bakers adding their own methods and tweaks to the genome. Here is something humbling I have discovered, too: a creation takes a particular flavour from its provenance. Lemon Squares from The Kitchen, made in those trays, in those ovens, look and taste completely different than when made in my home kitchen. I am humbled but at peace with this truth. The Kitchen's Lemon Squares live eternally as a myth.

But for a new time, a new Lemon Square! And, girl, are they puckery and amazing! These, adapted from Odette William's Instagram feed (@odettewilliams), have a wonderful chunkier base and the smoothest, curdiest lemon filling. I am bringing that citrus for you, lemophiles!

FOR THE CRUST

1½ cups all-purpose flour

½ cup oats

½ cup white sugar

¼ cup light brown sugar

¼ tsp bicarbonate of soda

¼ tsp salt

125 g butter, melted

FOR THE FILLING

5 large egg yolks, room temperature

1 can condensed milk

⅔ cup lemon juice

1 Tbsp grated lemon zest

1 Tbsp fresh thyme or lemon thyme (optional)

Preheat the oven to 180°C. You will need a baking tin of 20 × 20 × 4 cm.

Line the tin generously with baking paper so that you are comfortably able to lift the whole bake out of the pan to slice on a board later.

Using a food processor, pulse together the dry ingredients for the crust. Add the melted butter and pulse until just combined. The mixture will appear sandy. Press this rough shortbread into the prepared pan and bake for 15 minutes, until golden around the edges. Remove from the oven and allow to cool.

Meanwhile, make the filling. Whisk the egg yolks and condensed milk in a large mixing bowl for 2 minutes, or until light and fluffy. Add the lemon juice, zest and thyme (if using), and whisk to combine. Pour the filling over the cooled crust and bake for 15 minutes, or until it starts to puff ever so slightly around the edges. You want the filling to *just* set.

Remove the tart from the oven and allow to chill in the fridge in its tin for a minimum of 2 hours, before removing from the tin and cutting into squares.

MAKES 16–20 SQUARES

Aniseed Shortbread

Two things drew me to this recipe: one, I am a lazy person who does not necessarily enjoy cutting out cookies with a cookie cutter, and two, aniseed. Something of this fragrance seems reminiscent of my father's upbringing in 'the country' (the Moravian Mission Station of Genadendal), of mosbolletjies from country farmstalls and of my mother's aniseed raisin loaf. Another appeal: the possibility of a super-thin, crispy rolled-out wafer of shortbread. Surely this would be good? You can see for yourself by trying this buttery biscuit.

2 cups cake flour

⅓ cup cornflour

½ tsp salt

225 g butter, softened

½ cup light brown sugar, whizzed in a food processor to achieve the texture of castor sugar

1 tsp vanilla essence

1 egg white

1 tsp water

2 tsp anise (seeds)

¼ cup white sugar

Combine the flour, cornflour and salt in a medium-sized bowl, and whisk to combine. Set aside.

Using an electric or stand mixer, cream the butter and light brown sugar on medium-high speed for 3–4 minutes, until light and fluffy. Add the vanilla essence and beat until well combined, scraping the bowl down as you go along to make sure everything is well combined.

With your mixer on low speed, add the dry ingredients and beat until just combined. Scrape down the sides of the bowl again and fold the mixture a few times to make sure everything is well combined, at the same time thinking thoughts of lightness and airiness; do not overmix. Remove the dough from the bowl and divide in half, wrapping each piece in clingwrap and flattening into discs. Refrigerate for 1 hour or up to 3 days.

Lay out a lightly floured sheet of baking paper. Lay a disc of dough on the baking paper. Place another sheet of baking paper on top of the dough and roll it out into an oblong shape to your desired thickness. The size of the two sheets of baking paper between which your dough is sandwiched will aid your efforts. I manage to roll out my dough to a rough 52 cm × 27 cm oblong shape to fit onto my biggest baking sheet. Remove the top sheet of baking paper and prick the dough all over with a floured fork. Repeat with the second piece of dough on a new sheet of baking paper.

Slide the baking paper with the rolled-out dough onto a baking sheet and freeze for about 10 minutes, until firm.

Preheat the oven to 180°C.

Lightly beat the egg white with the water to thin it out. Brush the top of the dough with the egg white and sprinkle with the anise, gently pressing the seeds down into the dough to help them stick.

Bake for 15–17 minutes, until the dough turns a deep golden colour at the edges. Remove from the oven and sprinkle the sheet of shortbread generously with the white sugar.

You might like to serve this whole sheet of shortbread in the middle of a table for lucky people to break off a piece and dip in ice cream or coffee. What fun! Or, this is what I like to do: allow the shortbread to cool on the baking tray for 4 minutes or so. Then, using a sharp knife, cut the shortbread into 2½–3 cm wide wafers, taking care not to break them.

When they have cooled for another 5 minutes or so, using a fish slice, spatula or offset palette knife, lift the long shortbread wafers gently onto a cooling rack to cool completely. Place gently in an appropriately large tin or airtight container to store.

Aniseed shortbread is also great served across a bowl of home-made ice cream.

MAKES ± 32 SHORTBREAD BISCUIT WAFERS

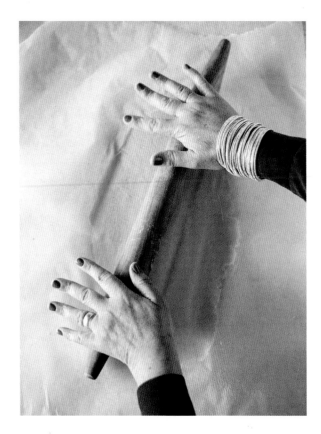

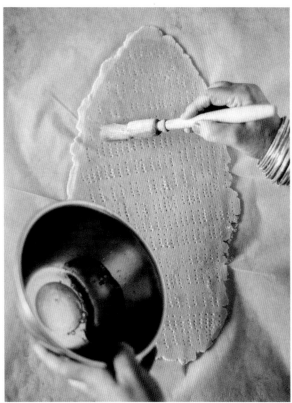
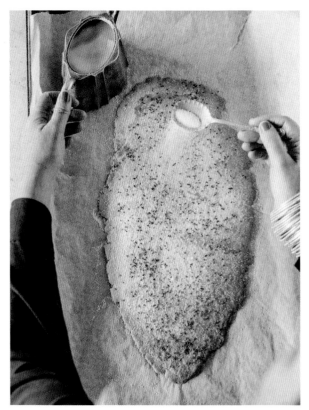

Best Chocolate Cake – really really! – with Great Chocolate Icing

I have been on a quest for the best (and easiest) chocolate cake to whip out quickly for any occasion: a birthday gift, a dessert for a party, or something for tea... What I have learned is that, often, people do not need a complex, dense, death-by-chocolate mud cake. A moist, tender, crumbed chocolate cake from an aunt is the one everyone longs for. Your quest ends here (thank you, Karen!). This is one of the most requested repeats from Karen's Box for Cooks!

2 cups cake wheat flour

2 cups white sugar

¾ cup cocoa powder

2 tsp baking powder

1½ tsp bicarbonate of soda

1 tsp salt

1 tsp instant coffee granules

1 cup buttermilk

½ cup sunflower oil

2 large eggs

2 tsp vanilla essence

1 cup boiling water

CHOCOLATE ICING

225 g soft butter

2½ cups icing sugar, sifted

⅔ cup cocoa powder, sifted

3 Tbsp milk

1 tsp vanilla essence

1 tsp instant coffee granules,
    dissolved in 2 tsp boiling water

NOTE:

As a fan of icing, I enjoy a good icing-to-cake ratio and prefer an iced, single-layer cake. The cake will go further this way, but for an impressive cake, sandwich away. If you need it to go the distance and still have a respectable slice of cake, make it a single!

Preheat the oven to 180°C. Cut out two circles of baking paper to cover the bottom of two 24 cm round, loose-bottomed cake tins. Grease and lightly flour the sides of the tins (or spray with non-stick baking spray).

To a large bowl or the bowl of a stand mixer, add the flour, sugar, cocoa powder, baking powder, bicarbonate of soda, salt and instant coffee. Whisk all these together.

Add the buttermilk, oil, eggs and vanilla essence to the dry ingredients, and mix on medium speed until well combined. Reduce the speed and carefully add the boiling water until the batter is well combined, but thin.

Divide the batter between the prepared cake tins. Bake for 30–35 minutes, until a skewer inserted into the centre of the cakes comes out clean. Remove from the oven and allow to cool slightly for 10 minutes. Turn the cakes out onto cooling racks to cool completely before sandwiching them together with the Chocolate Icing.

Beat the butter and icing sugar together until creamy, light and smooth. Add the cocoa powder, milk, vanilla and instant coffee, and beat to a creamy spreading consistency.

SERVES 8 PER SINGLE-LAYER CAKE (16 FOR 2 CAKES) AND 10 FOR A TRADITIONAL CAKE SANDWICH.

Tres Leches Cake
(and a Good Vanilla Sponge)

When my Sweetheart and I married in 2002, we had a huge party and squashed 200 people into our newly renovated home in Woodstock. A marquee covered the entire front garden, there were no chairs (only benches), a band of township kids played the best jazz, the Woodstock Starlights serenaded us down the road, and my girlfriends made huge crêpe flowers and garlands. Surrounded by all those we loved, it was the best party ever. My friend, Meg, and Mama Manzi helped cater everything! There was dancing. There was a piñata. And there was a Tres Leches Cake, a much more glamorous confection than the one I share here. (I did not get a tiny crumb of the wedding cake.) People swooned! Whenever I make this cake, there is much swooning, too. This cake too is a weapon of woo. Stand back carrot, granadilla and coffee cake, and yes, even chocolate cake. This is the winner!

FOR THE VANILLA SPONGE

200 g soft butter
¾ cup + 1 Tbsp (200 g) castor sugar
4 eggs at room temperature, beaten
1½ cups (200 g) self-raising flour
1 tsp baking powder
Tiny pinch of salt
2 Tbsp milk
1 tsp vanilla essence

FOR THE TRES LECHES

1 can Ideal milk (evaporated milk)
1 can condensed milk
1 cup fresh cream
Seeds scraped from 1 vanilla bean,
  or 1 tsp vanilla essence

NOTE:

To use this vanilla cake with other fillings such as icing or jam and cream, allow the cake to cool for 5 minutes in its tin, then turn out onto a wire rack to cool completely.

Preheat the oven to 180°C on the fan setting. Line the bottoms of two round 20 cm cake tins (or one 24 cm cake tin) with baking paper and spray the sides with non-stick baking spray, or butter and flour, to prevent sticking.

In the bowl of an electric stand mixer, cream the butter and sugar together until light and creamy. (This is the secret to a light, fluffy cake.) With the mixer on a medium speed, slowly add the beaten eggs until combined. Take the bowl from the stand and, with a large spatula, gently fold in the flour, baking powder and salt, alternating with the milk and vanilla essence. Transfer the batter to the prepared cake tins and bake for 20–25 minutes, until a skewer inserted into the centres comes out clean.

While the cakes are baking, whisk all the Tres Leches ingredients well toghether in a large jug. When the cakes come out of the oven, poke holes all over them with a skewer while in their tins. Slowly drizzle over the Tres Leches until it completely saturates the cakes.

This cake is most delicious when cold. Leave the soaked cakes a few hours in their tins in the fridge (or overnight).

MAKES 2 × 20 CM CAKES OR ONE LARGE 24 CM CAKE (SERVES 12 OR MORE)

Semolina Cake

In Istanbul we ate a semolina cake, revani, in a white-tiled basement restaurant packed with happy eaters. I will never forget it. The texture of this cake is delectable.

FOR THE SYRUP

2 cups white sugar

2 cups water

Juice and zest of 1 lemon

3 Tbsp rose water (optional)

FOR THE CAKE

3 eggs

¾ cup + 1 Tbsp castor sugar

¼ cup olive oil

225 g full-cream yoghurt

½ cup cake wheat flour

Pinch of salt

1 cup semolina

1 tsp vanilla essence

Juice of 1 lemon and zest of 2

1 tsp baking powder

24 whole almonds, to decorate (optional)

Make the syrup by combining the sugar, water, lemon juice and zest, and bring to a boil. Boil for 3 minutes, stirring constantly to dissolve the sugar, then remove from the heat, add the rose water (if using) and allow to cool.

Preheat the oven to 180°C. Line the bottom of a 30 × 22 cm baking tin with baking paper and spray the sides with non-stick baking spray.

To make the cake, beat the eggs on high speed in the bowl of a stand mixer. While you are doing so, add the castor sugar, little by little, until the mixture is light, about 4 minutes. Add the olive oil and yoghurt, and continue beating for about 1 minute to combine. Add the flour, salt, semolina, vanilla essence, lemon juice and zest, and beat for another minute until combined. Finally, mix in the baking powder.

Pour the mixture into the prepared baking tin and bake for 30–40 minutes. At 30 minutes, pull the cake from the oven and quickly press the almonds in even rows over the pale cake (think one almond per square portion). Pop the cake back in the oven for another 5–10 minutes until it is golden.

Remove the cake from the oven and pour the cooled syrup evenly over the cake. Allow it to soak into the cake completely. Once the cake has absorbed the syrup and cooled for 30 minutes, cover lightly and refrigerate in the tin for a few hours or overnight. It is delicious cold from the fridge.

SERVES 10 OR MORE

Lemon Poppy Seed Cake

During this at-home time, I felt compelled to make cake, to have a 'nice thing' for tea. My kids were so very fond of this cake, and so appreciative of my efforts, that this chef-mom felt a little remorse for having deprived them of these sorts of simple homely pleasures while hundreds of others in my work life were enjoying a small mountain of sweet treats daily. But this might just have been me overthinking. Ben and Maggie do not seem too bothered. With this cake, I celebrate my Mommy-ness.

FOR THE LEMON GLAZE
⅓ cup freshly squeezed lemon juice
⅓ cup (75 g) white sugar

FOR THE 'EXTRA' LEMON ICING (OPTIONAL)
In teenage speak it's *extra* but not embarrassing!

2 cups icing sugar, sifted
2 Tbsp freshly squeezed lemon juice
Zest of 1 lemon, finely grated
10 g salted butter, melted

FOR THE CAKE
⅓ cup milk
⅓ cup poppy seeds
1⅓ cups cake wheat flour
½ tsp bicarbonate of soda
1 tsp baking powder
¼ tsp salt
2 eggs
1 cup white sugar
Zest of 2 lemons, grated
½ tsp vanilla essence
¼ cup yoghurt
¾ cup sunflower oil

Preheat the oven to 160°C. Line a 30 × 11 cm loaf tin with baking paper. Allow a generous few centimetres above the tin to encourage the cake to rise to its full potential.

To make the glaze, bring the lemon juice and sugar to a simmer in a small pot, stirring constantly until the sugar dissolves. Remove from the heat and set aside to cool.

For the 'Extra' Lemon Icing, combine all the icing ingredients together in a large jug. Add a few more drops of lemon juice if you would like it to be runnier.

To make the cake, start by heating the milk and poppy seeds in a small pot over low heat. Bring to a gentle simmer then remove from the heat and allow to cool completely.

In a medium-sized bowl, whisk together the flour, bicarbonate of soda, baking powder and salt.

In the bowl of a stand mixer, whisk the eggs and sugar together until light and fluffy. Add the lemon zest, vanilla essence, yoghurt and sunflower oil, together with the cooled milk and poppy seeds.

With your mixer on a medium speed, slowly incorporate the dry-ingredient mixture into the wet mixture in two stages, mixing until just combined. Do not overmix. Pour the batter into the loaf tin and bake for 45–55 minutes until golden and a skewer inserted comes out clean. If the cake seems to be getting too dark, cover it with baking paper or tin foil. Once the cake is done, remove it from the oven and pour all the lemon glaze over the cake.

Once the cake is completely cool and the lemon glaze has been absorbed, remove the cake from its tin, place on a platter and drizzle over the Extra Lemon Icing, if using.

SERVES 8–10

Persian Granny's Pudding

If a Persian granny had served this pudding to me, I would have looked deep into her eyes and asked, 'How did you know? How did you know my darkest cravings? How could you have cast this spell on me? This spell of condensed milk and cream, almonds and pastry? Is this evil, sweet knowledge passed down from Ottoman palace kitchens?' It certainly has landed in mine, now adapted, from Sally Butcher's wonderful book, Meze. I am entranced because, between the cream and the sweetness, it reminds me of another favourite dish of the Cape, boeber.

1 can condensed milk

1 cup water

5 cardamom cloves, crushed

1 cinnamon stick

1 tsp vanilla essence

4 large plain croissants (they do not have to be special; cheap ones, even one- or two-day old ones will do)

¾ cup medium desiccated coconut

200 g nuts, toasted and chopped (one or more of these: whole almonds, pistachios, blanched hazelnuts, pine nuts or cashews)

1 cup cream, whipped to soft peaks

TO DECORATE

½ cup toasted almond flakes

½ cup toasted coconut flakes

¼ cup pistachio nuts, roughly chopped (optional)

2 tsp dried rose petals (optional)

Preheat the oven to 200°C.

Stir together the condensed milk, water, cardamom, cinnamon and vanilla essence in a small saucepan and gently bring the mixture to a boil. Lower the heat and simmer for about 5 minutes. Remove from the heat.

Tear up the croissants by hand and spread them over a large oven dish (20 × 30 × 3 cm) rubbed with butter. Sprinkle the desiccated coconut and the nuts over the torn croissants. Remove the spices from the condensed milk mixture (or not). Pour the condensed milk mixture over the croissants, being careful to not displace the coconut and nuts. Allow the croissants to absorb some of this liquid. Spoon the whipped cream over the whole pudding.

Bake the pudding for 15 minutes, or until the top is set and golden. Remove from the oven and decorate immediately with the toasted almond flakes and coconut flakes, as well as the pistachios and rose petals (if using), so that the toppings settle into the pudding. This pudding is great served warm. Let it cool for 5 minutes before serving. It will be extremely hot because of the high sugar content.

Happiness! Do you need some extra pouring cream (unsweetened!) beside this pudding? Perhaps. Serve small portions initially, so as not to overwhelm people with the heady sweetness!

SERVES 6

Ukrainian Yoghurt Pancakes or Little Doughnuts

It is amazing what you conjure up as a regular treat for a household (happily) trapped in their Woodstock home with two hapless dogs. What will they eat? Pancakes! Doughnuts! Often at all times of the day and night. Rules are tossed out of the window. Doughnuts at midnight? Doused in golden syrup? Why not! Pancakes for supper? Hang, let's do it! The puffy airiness in both offers deep comfort in moments of sadness, longing and confusion.

I gleaned this recipe from Mamushka by Olia Hercules. The Ukrainians understood a lot about austerity, resourcefulness and resilience from their assimilation into the Soviet bloc during Cold-War-era Russia. Turns out this recipe also creates the most heavenly little doughnuts when spooned into a hot wok and deep-fried. It is naughty and unnecessary but I drop blobs of butter onto the hot pile of doughnuts, drizzle them with moskonfyt or golden syrup, and then dust them with powdered sugar as well. Gosh. Austerity and then excess!

320 ml full-fat yoghurt

2 eggs, beaten

Pinch of fine salt

1½ cups cake wheat flour

1 tsp baking soda

3–4 cups sunflower oil, for deep-frying
(doughnuts) OR ¼ cup sunflower oil,
for frying (pancakes)

OPTIONAL TOPPINGS

30 g butter (optional)

Golden syrup, to taste

Powdered sugar, for dusting

Preheat the oven to 150°C. Have a baking sheet ready to pop into the oven to keep the pancakes warm.

Combine all the ingredients (except the oil) and mix until you have a mostly-smooth batter. The batter will be stiffer than you might be accustomed to with flapjacks or American pancakes.

For little doughnuts, heat the oil in a wok over medium-high heat. Drop teaspoonsful of the batter into the hot oil. Turn the doughnuts in the oil so that they fry 1–2 minutes on each side. When cooked and golden-brown, remove and transfer to a tray lined with paper towel. Drop little knobs of butter over the cooked doughnuts, drizzle with golden syrup and dust generously with icing sugar.

For pancakes, heat the oil in a heavy-bottomed pan. Once hot, drop generous dessertspoonsful into the oil, frying gently on both sides until golden and cooked through. These pancakes are exceptionally light and puffy. If you are worried whether they are cooked through, pop them onto a warm baking sheet as they come out of the pan; they will continue to cook gently as you fry all the pancakes.

Serve them hot with all the toppings your family desires.

**MAKES A PILE OF ± 40 LITTLE DOUGHNUTS
OR 24–30 PANCAKES, DEPENDING ON THEIR SIZE
(SERVES 4–5 GREEDY PEOPLE)**

[12]

The new imagination

It requires a concerted energy to imagine something new. It requires identifying our dead, crusty, old ideas that were not working or serving a broader people. It takes a shaking off, peeling off, of old definitions. And, always, there is the temptation to return to old ways of doing things.

There's been a break, a time for reflection.

Our lives have been disrupted and we are learning that this could be a good thing.

Things that matter have been brought into focus, a lot of the noise momentarily cleared.

We can use this opportunity, even as it unfolds, to choose how we will live *now*. We can choose simplicity. We can seek out the beauty in the everyday (oh, the folds of this cabbage!). We can stop platitudes. We can understand that our reality might be *not knowing* and we can be patient with each other as we figure out how we will live now. We can choose to be kinder to ourselves, our families, and the people we call our community. We can listen harder. We can pay attention. We can stay with the understanding, the very un-Western mindset, that *we have enough*. And it is good. And we can be content. We can stay open, curious and learning, rather than resigned and conceited.

Let's use everything we have in our fridges – carrot tops and parsley stalks. Let's grow lettuce and tomatoes and herbs, and plant fruit trees in our gardens and in our local parks. Let's make a supper of vegetables. Eat leftovers for breakfast and lunch. We can be committed locavores and support small farmers and local industries. Let's champion community projects and distribution centres. Let's have conversations with kids around our tables. Let's look for the anomalous and the unexpected. Let's experiment and collaborate – this is the way we will shape and reinvent our world.

Index

Acknowledgements and thanks

When I closed my restaurant there was an enormous outpouring of grief and sadness. Friends from all over South Africa and the world expressed their love and friendship with messages, poems and support. I felt carried on this warm sea of friendship. I understood that we had made something extraordinary at The Kitchen, that I had done something good! Amid tremendous turmoil and loss, this affirmation directed my trajectory powerfully onwards. In my head, learnings and ideas to share and employ. In my heart, love.

And so now I pour out my heart of grateful thanks to all the friends of The Kitchen, folk who stood in queues, crowded at benches, waiting for Love Sandwiches, Broccoli Soffriti and Honey Mustard Sausages. What a delicious time we had! WE made a beautiful space together. Thank you. This book is for you. Come with me as we move Onwards!

My enormous thanks to all who donated money to my crew. You cannot begin to know what your generosity meant at that time. Thank you to Jacana Media who gave portions of the sale of my first book to my Kitchen family. Thank you to UCook and Granadilla Eats for the platform to earn and so pay my people.

Putting this book together was a joy, start to finish! Phatiswa Magazi, formerly head of kitchen at The Kitchen, was by my side the whole way. We cooked, tested, and tasted again and again. I experienced that peculiar joy of cooking as we did at The Kitchen. Phati's rigour and attention kept us proficient. Kudakwashe and I packed up The Kitchen by ourselves, and Kuda was with me again as we did all the preparation for shooting *Onwards*. Thank you Phati and Kuda.

It is a rare thing to be able to work with creatives who 'get you' and who are masters of their craft. Roxy Spears (art direction) and Claire Gunn (photography) revelled in my (now righteous) collection of fabrics, ceramics and china as my home became a veritable prop shop while we shot *Onwards*. Can you see all the fun we had? Thank you, Roxy, for corralling us and for lending your eye and craft towards the *Onwards* movement! Thank you, Claire, for the energy and artistic passion you brought to our enterprise.

My huge thanks to Beverley Dodd of Penguin Random House for making *Onwards* possible, and for guiding our endeavours with vision and kindness. Aimee Carelse, my editor, was thorough and patient, and Randall Watson put it all together. What a fine team. Thank you for your exceptional attention.

My teenagers, Ben and Maggie, were incredibly gracious during the making of this book. They showed restraint amid piles of plates and fabrics, and a fridge (even more) full of potions, their mother in sparkly-eyed feverish distraction. They were hand models and reflector holders. Thank you, Ben, for 'carrying the weight of the Karen Dudley social-media brand' on your breaking back!

When I married my Sweetheart, David, I knew my life would be better with him in it. Twenty something years later, I cannot imagine any journey without him.

The defining experience at the diamond-hard centre of reality is the eternal movement as beautiful and fearful invitation: a beckoning dynamic, asking us to move from this to that.

–From the chapter, 'Pilgrim', in *Consolations* by David Whyte (Many Rivers Press). Please go ahead and read the whole book!